Standards-Based
LANGUAGE ARTS
Graphic Organizers, Rubrics, and Writing Prompts for Middle Grade Students

By Imogene Forte
and Sandra Schurr

Incentive Publications, Inc.
Nashville, Tennessee

Graphics by Joe Shibley
Cover by Marta Drayton
Edited by Jean K. Signor

ISBN 0-86530-492-0

PRINTED IN THE UNITED STATES OF AMERICA
www.incentivepublications.com

Table of Contents

PREFACE

Recent research studies have confirmed a belief that intuitive teachers have long held germane to classroom success; when students are meaningfully involved in active learning tasks and in the planning and evaluation of their work, they are more enthusiastic about instructional activities, they learn and retain more, and their overall rate of achievement is greater. With the emphasis placed on measurable achievement as an overriding goal driving school system mandates, curriculum, classroom organization and management, and even instructional practices and procedures, teachers are faced with great challenges. While striving to fulfill societal demands, at the same time they must be creating and using new instructional strategies, procedures, and teaching methods to meet the diverse needs of students with widely varying interests and abilities. With the complexity of daily life in the rapidly changing world in which we live, the global economy, and the growing avalanche of information, middle grades language arts teachers are turning to student-centered instruction, active learning strategies, and authentic instruction to capture and hold students' interests and attention, and consequently to result in increased achievement levels.

Graphic Organizers

As the body of material to be covered in a given time frame grows more massive and multifaceted, and content demands on students and teachers multiply, graphic organizers are becoming an important component of middle grades language arts programs.

In the information-saturated classroom of today, sorting and making meaningful use of specific facts, and concepts is becoming an increasingly important skill. Knowing where to go to find information and how to organize it once it is located is the key to processing and making meaningful use of the information gathered. Graphic organizers can be used to: provide visual organization; develop scope and sequence; furnish a plan of action or to aid in assessment; clarify points of interest; and document a process or a series of events.

Their construction and use encourages visual discrimination and organization, use of critical thinking skills, and meta-cognitive reflection. They can be particularly useful in helping middle grade students grasp concepts and skills related to the twelve standards established by the National Council of Teachers of English.

In other instances, a graphic organizer may be developed as a reporting or review exercise or sometimes as a means of self-assessment when properly used after knowledge has been acquired. Graphic organizers become a valuable and effective instructional and assessment tool. The degree of their effectiveness for both students and teachers is determined by visual clarification of purpose, careful planning, visual organization, and attention to detail.

Rubrics

Authentic assessment, as opposed to more traditional forms of assessment, gives both student and teacher a more realistic picture of gains made, facts, and information processed for retention. Emphasis is placed more on the processing of concepts and information than on the recall of facts. Collecting evidence from authentic assessment exercises, taking place in realistic settings over a period of time, provides students and teachers with the most effective documentation of both skills and content mastery. Traditional measurements of student achievement such as written tests and quizzes, objective end-of-chapter tests, and standardized tests play a major role in the assessment picture as well.

The use of standards-based rubrics in middle grade language arts classes has proven to be an extremely useful means of authentic assessment for helping students maintain interest and evaluate their own progress.

Rubrics are checklists that contain sets of criteria for measuring the elements of a product, performance, or portfolio. They can be designed as a qualitative measure (holistic rubric) to gauge overall performance of a prompt, or they can be designed as a quantitative measure (analytic rubric) to award points for each of several elements in response to a prompt.

Additional benefits from rubrics are that they: require collaboration among students and teachers; are flexible and allow for individual creativity; make room for individual strengths and weaknesses; minimize competition; are meaningful to parents; allow for flexible time frames; provide multifaceted scoring systems with a variety of formats; can be sources for lively peer discussions and interaction; can include meta-cognitive reflection provisions which encourage self-awareness and critical thinking; and can help teachers determine final grades that are understood by and hold meaning for students.

Writing Prompts

Over the past several years, the significance of journals and writing prompts is well-documented by student and teacher observations. When students write about experiences, knowledge, hopes, fears, memories, and dreams, they broaden and clarify skills and concepts while acquiring new insights into themselves and the big world of which they are a part.

While random journal entries hold their own place of importance in the language arts classroom, writing prompts designed to elicit specific responses play a vital role in the instructional program.

Journal entries may be presented in many different formats, and may be shared and assessed in a variety of ways. The flexibility of their use and the possibility they provide for integrating instruction cause them to be viewed as an important component of the personalized language arts program. They may take the form of a file card project, a multimedia presentation, a special notebook, or a diary. They may be private to be discussed with the teacher only, shared with a small group of peers, or the total class. Word prompts can be used in parent-student-teacher conferences, or as take home projects to be shared with parents, saved, or used as a portfolio entry to give an account of a unit of study, field trip, or independent project.

Writing prompts provide the opportunity for students to: create a dialogue with teachers in meaningful sense; write about self-selected topics of high interest; process and internalize material being learned; communicate with peers; express private opinions, thoughts, and insights without judgment or censor; write personal reactions or responses to textbook, research assignments, group discussion, and experiences; make record of what and how they are learning and what it means to them; develop a source book of ideas and thoughts related to a specific topic; question material being studied and record answers as they are uncovered; assess their academic or social progress; and engage in meta-cognitive reflection on new skills and concepts being acquired and record plans for further exploration.

These standards-based graphic organizers, writing prompts, and rubrics have been designed to provide busy teachers with a bank of resources from which to draw as the need arises. The twelve standards developed by the National Council of Teachers of English and the International Reading Association have been incorporated throughout all activities. For ease in planning, the matrix on page 128 provides a complete correlation of activities to these standards.

Graphic Organizers

Idea
Idea
Idea
SubTopic

Idea
Idea
Idea
Idea
SubTopic

SubTopic

Main Topic

SubTopic

SubTopic

SubTopic

Idea

POINT FIVE:
POINT FOUR:
PROBLEM:
POINT ONE:
POINT TWO:

GETTING READY FOR THE INTERVIEW

Name of Interviewee_____

Name of Interviewer_____

Date of Interview_____

Purpose of Interview_____

CONDUCTING THE INTERVIEW

Question One_____

Response_____

Question One_____

Response_____

Question One_____

Response_____

FOLLOWING THE INTERVIEW

Results of Interview _____

GUIDELINES

For Using Graphic Organizers

1. Graphic organizers have many purposes: they can be used for curriculum planning, helping students process information, and pre- or post-assessment tasks. Determine which types of graphic organizers are best for each purpose.

2. Graphic organizers are a performance-based model of assessment and make excellent artifacts for inclusion in a portfolio. Decide which concepts in your discipline are best represented by the use of these organizers.

3. Use graphic organizers to help students focus on important concepts while omitting extraneous details.

4. Use graphic organizers as visual pictures to help the student remember key ideas.

5. Use graphic organizers to connect visual language with verbal language in active learning settings.

6. Use graphic organizers to enhance recall of important information.

7. Use graphic organizers to provide student motivation and relieve student boredom.

8. Use graphic organizers to show and explain relationships between and among varied content areas.

9. Use graphic organizers to make traditional lesson plans more interactive and more appealing to the visual learner.

10. Use graphic organizers to break down complex ideas through concise and structured visuals.

11. Use graphic organizers to help students note patterns and clarify ideas.

12. Use graphic organizers to help students better understand the concept of part to whole.

13. Emphasize the use of graphic organizers to stimulate creative thinking.

14. Make sure there is a match between the type of organizer and the content being taught.

15. Make sure that using a graphic organizer is the best use of time when teaching a concept.

16. Use a wide variety of graphic organizers and use them collaboratively whenever possible.

Standards-Based LANGUAGE ARTS Graphic Organizers, Rubrics, and Writing Prompts for Middle Grade Students

Copyright ©2001 by Incentive Publications, Inc. Nashville, TN.

Author's Life Story

The Author's Life Story figure may be used to record important information about an author. It will be useful as a tool for organizing data collected from several sources about the life and work of an author of particular interest or for gathering material for a report on a famous person, media personality, or community leader.

See page 27 for reproducible copy.

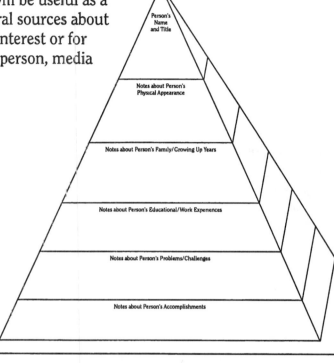

Person's Name and Title

Notes about Person's Physical Appearance

Notes about Person's Family/Growing Up Years

Notes about Person's Educational/Work Experiences

Notes about Person's Problems/Challenges

Notes about Person's Accomplishments

Autobiography or Biography Organizer

The Autobiography Organizer is useful for organizing major facts of a specific life story. It may be used by students as a writing and for sorting out information and events related to their own lives in preparation for writing their own autobiography. The same graphic organization applies to the study of the biography of a famous person. This is especially true when study allows for use of a variety of resource materials that need to be clarified and coordinated to provide interest, as well as eliminate overlap or redundancy of facts and information.

See page 28 for reproducible copy.

An Autobiography or Biography of:	
Place/Date of Birth	
Family History	
Early Life	
Education	
Major Action	
Major Events	
Major Influences	
Major Contributors	
Major Friends	
Major Problems	
Famous Quotes or Words	

Standards-Based LANGUAGE ARTS Graphic Organizers, Rubrics, and Writing Prompts for Middle Grade Students

Bloom's Taxonomy
Book Report Pyramid

The Bloom's Taxonomy Book Report Pyramid can serve as a valuable tool for students when organizing their thoughts about a book they have read.

This pyramid encourages students to: evaluate, synthesize, analyze, apply, comprehend, and become knowledgeable about the material they have read before assembling it into a written, oral, or graphic book report.

See page 29 for reproducible copy.

Title: _____
Author: _____
Publisher: _____ Date: _____
Evaluation

Synthesis

Analysis

Application

Comprehension

Knowledge

Bloom's Taxonomy
Bridge of Knowledge Organizer

The Bloom's Taxonomy Bridge of Knowledge Organizer will be useful as a student planning form for a specific content lesson, a research project, a group unit, or enrichment project. The value of this organizer is the capacity it affords for the entire plan to be shown in a concise manner on one page: topic, plan, resources needed and their location, student required date of completion, and dates of student and teacher comments.

See page 30 for reproducible copy.

Application	Analogy
Comprehension	Synthesis
Knowledge	Evaluation

Book Report Ladder

The book report graphic organizer can serve as a valuable organizational tool for middle grade students of all ages. When properly presented, this organizational procedure encourages critical thinking in that material must be summarized and synthesized in order to fit into the limited spacing, use of plot and sequence, recall selection, and reflection skills.

The same framework be useful as a planning tool for creative or process writing. It may also be used to develop a report on a biography of a famous person, a factual documentary report of a historical event or social movement of a play, movie, or video depicting any of the above. Students should be encouraged to report the facts and important information as accurately as possible while at the same time employing original illustrations, timelines, story webs, or other details to make the report as graphically interesting and informative as possible.

See page 31 for reproducible copy.

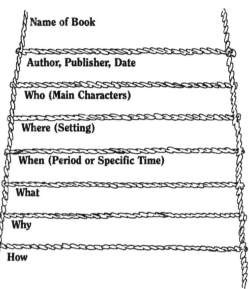

Name of Book

Author, Publisher, Date

Who (Main Characters)

Where (Setting)

When (Period or Specific Time)

What

Why

How

Cause-and-Effect Chain

A series of cause-and-effect relationships learned from a topic of study or from a book may be recorded in the appropriate sections of the cause-and-effect chain to chart the order of a course of events.

When care is taken to record the events accurately, the chain will show that each CAUSE produces a related EFFECT and that all of the CAUSES lead to the ultimate or final EFFECT.

See page 32 for reproducible copy.

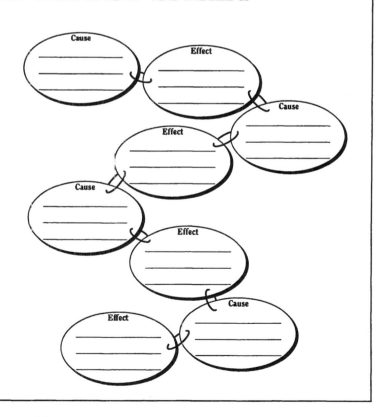

Character Analysis Web

A character analysis web presents biographical information, the personality traits, actions, and accomplishments of a main or supporting character from a novel, short story, textbook, or a newspaper or magazine article. Important pieces of information are recorded on the outline of the character as a visual record of the person's accomplishments, words, actions, and/or deeds.

See page 33 for reproducible copy.

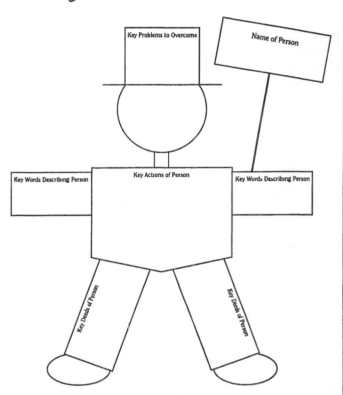

Compare and Contrast

This organizer is used to relate a newly acquired concept to prior learned knowledge related to the concept. Concept 1 and Concept 2 should be recorded in the two rectangles at the top of the page.

Comparison step: Write how the two concepts are similar in the *How Alike?* box.

Contrast Step: Note the differences between the two concepts in the *How Different?* columns.

See page 34 for reproducible copy.

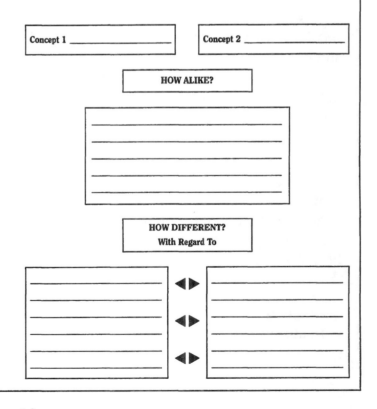

14

Concept Map

The concept map can be especially helpful for showing a series of events from a novel, novella, biography, play, or social studies reading assignment. It is built around a central concept important to the study of a given topic. Other facts or insights related to the main idea in some meaningful way are recorded as extensions or associations of the main concept through a series of adjacent lines and circles.

See page 35 for reproducible copy.

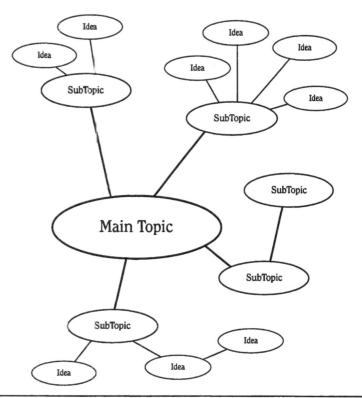

Cycle Organizer

The Cycle Organizer can be used to identify events that tend to be circular or cyclical in nature. The book or topic title is written in the title circle. The events or situations that must take place, in sequence to complete the cycle successfully are then listed in the oval circles.

The first event or situation should be recorded at the top circle, with subsequent events recorded in the other circles, moving in a clockwise direction. Additional circles may be inserted anywhere in the cycle as needed.

See page 36 for reproducible copy.

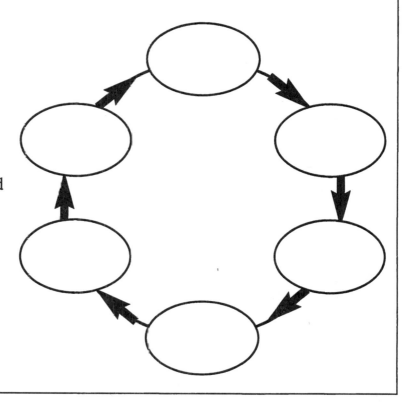

Easy-to-Make Cube Report

Since cubes have six sides and information can be recorded on all six sides, the cube offers a unique format for using Bloom's Taxonomy to organize and present an interesting and informative report. Cubes can be constructed from existing boxes in various sizes, or from boxes made from poster board or oak tag. If printed cardboard boxes are used, they should be covered with paper so that the recorded information will be easy to read and study.

There are four steps in developing a cube report:

1. Select a topic.

2. Do research on the topic. Summarize, and organize it according to Bloom's Taxonomy. For information on Bloom's Taxonomy, see pages 28, 29, and 139.

3. Construct the cube.

4. Print or type the information on poster or typing paper, and paste the information on the six sides of the cube.

A cube may be made by covering a box with butcher paper or wrapping paper, or building a new cube using the pattern provided on the next page. If the second option is selected, enlarge the cube pattern so that the report will be more readable.

Note: The cube lends itself especially well to book reports. When colorful graphics are added, the completed cube makes an interesting art object to remind the reader of an enjoyable reading experience. For a Cube Report Assessment Rubric, see page 97.

See page 37 for reproducible copy.

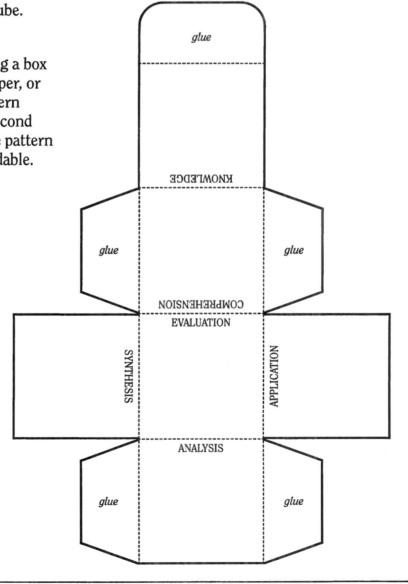

Fact and Information Organizer

Use the facts and information organizer to record information and structure your ideas on a topic on any content area. The major topic is written in the oval at the top of the tree, subheadings in the smaller ovals, and facts and information on the diagonal lines extending from the subheadings. This graphic organizer is especially useful for organizing and making meaningful use of a vast and unwieldy amount of information on a given subject.

See page 38 for reproducible copy.

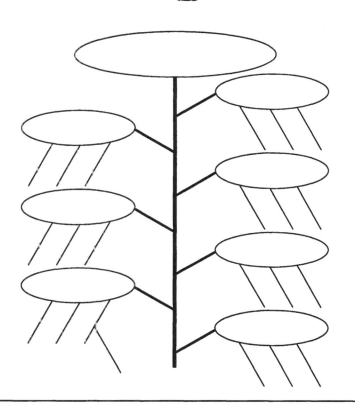

Group Report Mural Plan

A mural report can be an interesting alternative for the traditional format most often used for chapter books, biographies, or content-based documentaries. It may be completed by a small group of students who create a mural as a collaborative report; it may be completed by one student as an individual report, or by two students who choose to use it as a product for authentic assessment of a peer tutoring study project. If it is used for a group report, the group decides on a topic, assigns different research tasks to each group member, and cooperatively outlines both the information and the illustrations to be included in the mural. Individuals or peer tutoring teams follow the same procedure with appropriate modifications.

See page 39 for reproducible copy.

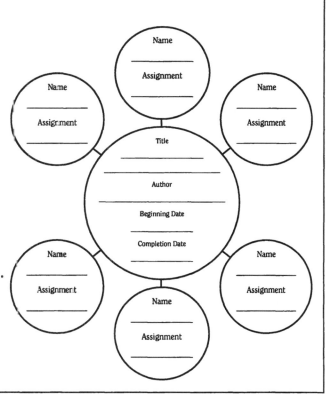

Standards-Based LANGUAGE ARTS Graphic Organizers, Rubrics, and Writing Prompts for Middle Grade Students

Individual Project Plan

Use this form to clarify assignments, dates, materials needed, goals, and a plan of action when beginning an individual learning project. This visual approach to planning can be extremely helpful for many students.

See page 40 for reproducible copy.

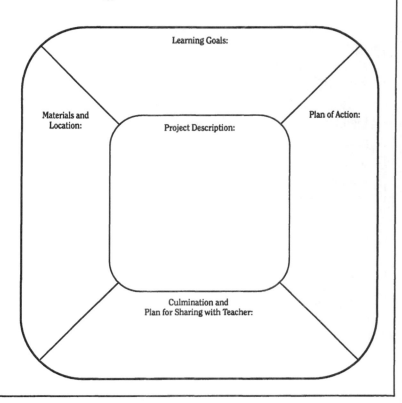

Learning Goals:

Materials and Location:

Project Description:

Plan of Action:

Culmination and Plan for Sharing with Teacher:

Interview Organizer

The interview organizer is designed to plan an upcoming interview with a person of interest. It is based on a set of questions asked by the interviewer with spaces provided for recording the interviewee's responses. Answers to the questions may then be used to structure the interview.

See page 41 for reproducible copy.

GETTING READY FOR THE INTERVIEW

Name of Interviewee_____
Name of Interviewer_____
Date of Interview_____
Purpose of Interview_____

CONDUCTING THE INTERVIEW

Question One_____
Response_____
Question One_____
Response_____
Question One_____
Response_____

FOLLOWING THE INTERVIEW

Results of Interview _____

18

Literature Analysis Stairway

Follow the steps on the stairway to analyze the major parts of a short story, novel, or poem. Note details, descriptions, events, clue words, traits, attributes, or ideas that summarize elements of the piece of literature. Review your notes on the other steps to help write a definitive statement summarizing the ending.

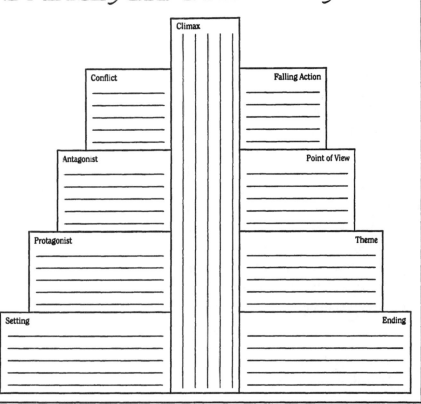

See page 42 for reproducible copy.

Observation Log

An observation log is a collection of simple, but informative entries about a given topic or subject. Observation logs are used to guide observation of a person, place, or thing over a period of time and to record the changes describe the observed event or action. Entries include the date and time of the observation.

See page 43 for reproducible copy.

Points to Ponder Star

Points to Ponder encourages students to consider various points or solutions to a specific problem under study. The problem is written in the center of the star and the key points to consider or potential solutions to the problem are written on the five points of the star. The Points to Ponder Star can be used to gather information for a content-based report, to pinpoint questions resulting from a textbook reading assignment, or to organize main issues and information for a research project.

See page 44 for reproducible copy.

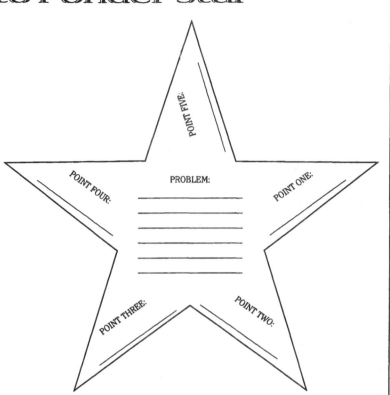

Portfolio Planning Guide

The portfolio contains a collection of artifacts reflecting the interests and the students efforts related to a designated content discipline or specific topic. It should contain a variety of items of different natures and may include writing samples, photographs, field experiences, and reports, interviews, graphics, and both product and performance notes and reflections. The portfolio planning guide, when carefully completed, will serve as a valuable reference tool.

See page 45 for reproducible copy.

Prediction Web

The Prediction Web is a valuable tool for organizing facts and information to deduce or support a prediction. Write the major topic or problem under discussion as a question in the square box at the bottom of the tree. Brainstorm possible predictions or probable outcomes in response to the question and record these in the prediction boxes. On the proof lines, record facts that either support or negate the predictions. This organizer can be used when studying a current event such as an election, sporting event, decision-making process, etc. Or it may be useful in the character analysis of the protagonist in a book.

See page 46 for reproducible copy.

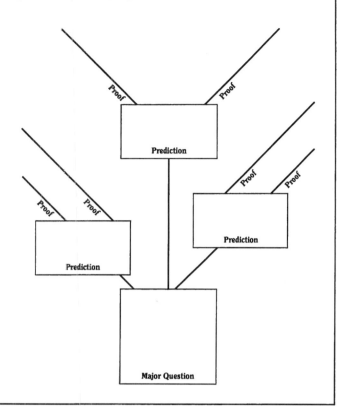

Project Tree Planning Tool

The Project Tree is useful as a tool for planning and completing a project based on a major goal and sub goals to be accomplished through the completion of a variety of sequential tasks. The major goal is written in the large box, the sub goals in the medium-sized boxes. The sequences of tasks are then organized in the smaller boxes. It is important that each set of tasks be grouped with the appropriate sub goal in the diagram.

See page 47 for reproducible copy.

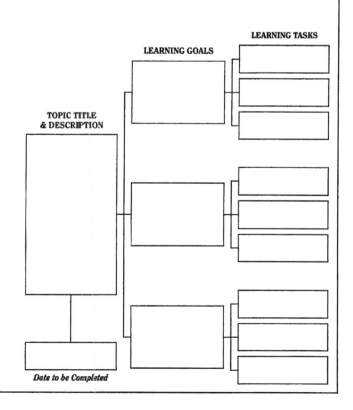

Standards-Based LANGUAGE ARTS Graphic Organizers,
Rubrics, and Writing Prompts for Middle Grade Students

Puzzle Grid

This grid is used for constructing crossword puzzles or word find puzzles. When designing a crossword puzzle, make a list of clues for words, write the words in appropriate squares on the grid, and black in the blank squares. When constructing a word find puzzle, use a separate piece of paper to list words related to a theme or topic. Fill appropriate squares with letters that form these words, and then add other letters at random to the blank squares.

See page 48 for reproducible copy.

Reporter's Template

The sequence of events as presented in the Reporter's Template illustrates the relative importance of the various components of an article written by a journalist. This information and procedure may also be used for creating a television documentary or advertisement. Since news articles must be written immediately after an event occurs in order to appear in print in a timely manner, it is of the utmost importance that the article is written quickly yet accurately. Therefore, the template can be a valuable organizational tool when properly used.

See page 49 for reproducible copy.

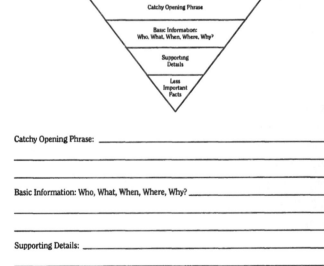

Catchy Opening Phrase: _____

_____

Basic Information: Who, What, When, Where, Why? _____

_____

_____

Supporting Details: _____

_____

Less Important Facts: _____

_____

_____

Research Study Plan

This planning form may be used to map out a game plan for completing an independent study of a specific topic, of an author's work, or a current event of particular significance. Since this planning form is flexible in nature to allow for individual creativity, it is important that specific details and plans for completing the study be recorded.

See page 50 for reproducible copy.

PERSONAL PROJECT PLAN

| Title and Description of Study | Beginning Date _____ Completion Date _____ | Format for Study |

Resources Needed and Location

Challenges to be expected and/or questions to answer

Method of Evaluation

Scope and Sequence Chart

The Scope and Sequence chart is useful for creating a timeline, organizing a sequence of events, or outlining a series of steps to perform a task. In the first box, write the first date, event, or step of the task. In the second box, write the second date, event, or step of the task. Continue in this way with the third, fourth, and fifth boxes. Additional boxes may be used if there is need for more stages in your planning.

See page 51 for reproducible copy.

Historical Setting

Historical Figures

Historical Problem Situation

First Event/Step: _____

Second Event/Step: _____

Third Event/Step: _____

Fourth Event/Step: _____

Fifth Event/Step: _____

Outcomes: _____

Resolution: _____

Standards-Based LANGUAGE ARTS Graphic Organizers, Rubrics, and Writing Prompts for Middle Grade Students

Graphic Organizer

Story Board

Storyboards are valuable for presenting a sequence of events in chronological order. They are particularly useful for studying a novel, historical event, or geographical exploration. They are also helpful for organizing information, ideas, thoughts or situations based on when and how they occurred or on their unique application to the topic under investigation. For Chalk Talk Report Assessment Rubric based on the Story Board Organizer, see page 94.

See page 52 for reproducible copy.

1.	6.
2.	7.
3.	8.
4.	9.
5.	10.

Graphic Organizer

SQ3R Chart

SURVEY: Read titles/subtitles. Notice words/phrases in special type. Skim illustrations/charts/graphs. Review end-of-chapter summaries and questions.

QUESTION: Turn main/subtopics in special print into 5W questions—Who, What, When, Where, and Why.

READ: Read information to answer questions, highlight main ideas, and make notes.

RECITE: Pause at the end of each chapter section to orally answer questions, using your own words.

REVIEW: Summarize main ideas from your reading.

See page 53 for reproducible copy.

Directions
This chart is helpful when reading a chapter from a textbook. Use one chart for each major section of the chapter. Remember that SQ3R means:

Survey: Read titles/subtitles. Notice words/phrases in special type. Skim illustrations/charts/graphs. Review end-of-chapter summaries and questions.

Question: Turn main/subtopics in special print into 5W questions—Who, What, When, Where, and Why.

Read: Read information to answer questions, highlighting main ideas and taking notes.

Recite: Pause at the end of each chapter section to answer questions orally, using your own words.

Review: Construct a study guide sheet that includes summaries and main ideas from your reading.

Survey: Record most important titles and subtitles from major chapter section.

Question: Write Who, What, When, Where, and Why questions for main/subtopics.

Read: Write short answers to five questions from above.

Standards-Based LANGUAGE ARTS Graphic Organizers, Rubrics, and Writing Prompts for Middle Grade Students

Copyright ©2001 by Incentive Publications, Inc. Nashville, TN.

The 5 Ws and How Web

The 5 Ws and How Web may be used to record the 5 Ws and How of a magazine article, a newspaper article, or an excerpt from a classroom textbook. Write the article or chapter titles in the center hexagon and answer the questions about the situation in the appropriate web sections. Then create a paragraph summarizing the information from this web.

See page 54 for reproducible copy.

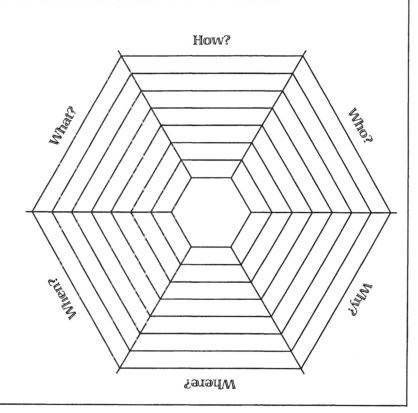

The Umbrella Organizer

The Umbrella graphic organizer is especially helpful for organizing thoughts and ideas for a topical report or essay. The main idea or concept is written inside the umbrella outline in two or three sentences. On the lines adjacent to the handle of the umbrella, write as many details or related thoughts as possible. These may be prioritized in some way, such as putting the major details on the side of the handle and the minor details on the other side of the handle. Or, a number scale might be used to order the ideas from most important to least important.

See page 55 for reproducible copy.

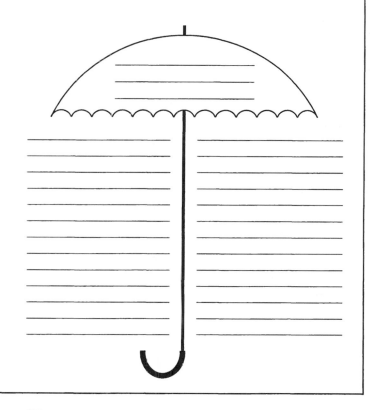

Standards-Based LANGUAGE ARTS Graphic Organizers, Rubrics, and Writing Prompts for Middle Grade Students

Vocabulary Learning Ladder

The Vocabulary Learning Ladder is useful in helping students to learn new words that they discover in their reading. On each step of the ladder, write a new word, the sentence in which the word was found, and the definition of the word.

See page 56 for reproducible copy.

Word or Term: _____
Textbook Sentence: _____
Page: _____ Definition: _____
_____
5

Word or Term: _____
Textbook Sentence: _____
Page: _____ Definition: _____
_____
4

Word or Term: _____
Textbook Sentence: _____
Page: _____ Definition: _____
_____
3

Word or Term: _____
Textbook Sentence: _____
Page: _____ Definition: _____
_____
2

Word or Term: _____
Textbook Sentence: _____
Page: _____ Definition: _____
_____
1

What, So What, Now What?

A What, So What, Now What? Chart organizes facts and provides meta-cognitive reflection related to the reading of a story, textbook section, newspaper, or magazine article on a topic.

The *What?* column requires the student to record a response to the question: *What is the meaning of this piece and/or what did I learn from it?*

The *So What?* column requires the student to record a series of responses to the question: *What difference does it make now that I know this, or what is its importance?*

The *Now What?* column asks students to record an answer to the question: *How can I use this information to make a difference in what I know or can do, or how is it important and relates to the major theme?*

See page 57 for reproducible copy.

Topic of Study _____

Student's Name _____

What?	So What?	Now What?

Author's Life Story

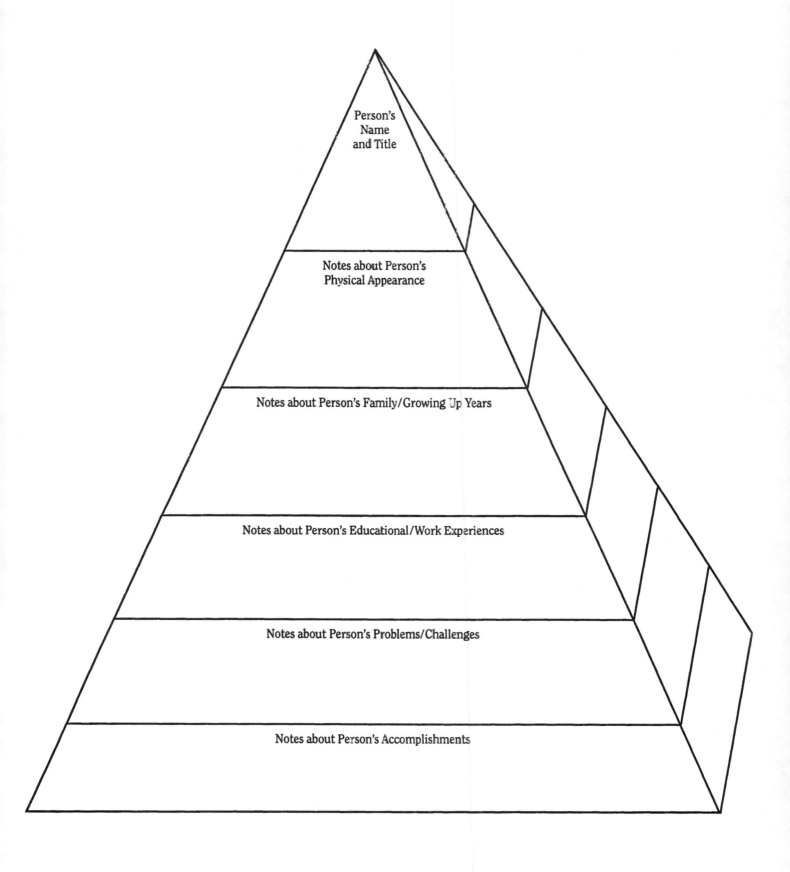

Person's
Name
and Title

Notes about Person's
Physical Appearance

Notes about Person's Family/Growing Up Years

Notes about Person's Educational/Work Experiences

Notes about Person's Problems/Challenges

Notes about Person's Accomplishments

*Standards-Based LANGUAGE ARTS Graphic Organizers,
Rubrics, and Writing Prompts for Middle Grade Students*

Autobiography or Biography Organizer

An Autobiography or Biography of:	
Place/Date of Birth	
Family History	
Early Life	
Education	
Major Action	
Major Events	
Major Influences	
Major Contributors	
Major Friends	
Major Problems	
Famous Quotes or Words	

Bloom's Taxonomy
Book Report Pyramid

Title: _____

Author: _____

Publisher: _____ Date: _____

Evaluation

Synthesis

Analysis

Application

Comprehension

Knowledge

Name _____ Date _____

Standards-Based LANGUAGE ARTS Graphic Organizers,
Rubrics, and Writing Prompts for Middle Grade Students

Bloom's Taxonomy
Bridge of Knowledge Organizer

Application	Analogy

Comprehension		Synthesis

Knowledge		Evaluation

Topic _____

Resources Needed _____

Resource Location _____

Completion Date _____

Student Signature: _____ Date: _____

Teacher Signature: _____ Date: _____

Standards-Based LANGUAGE ARTS Graphic Organizers,
Rubrics, and Writing Prompts for Middle Grade Students

Book Report Ladder

Name of Book

Author, Publisher, Date

Who (Main Characters)

Where (Setting)

When (Period or Specific Time)

What

Why

How

31

*Standards-Based LANGUAGE ARTS Graphic Organizers,
Rubrics, and Writing Prompts for Middle Grade Students*

Cause-and-Effect Chain

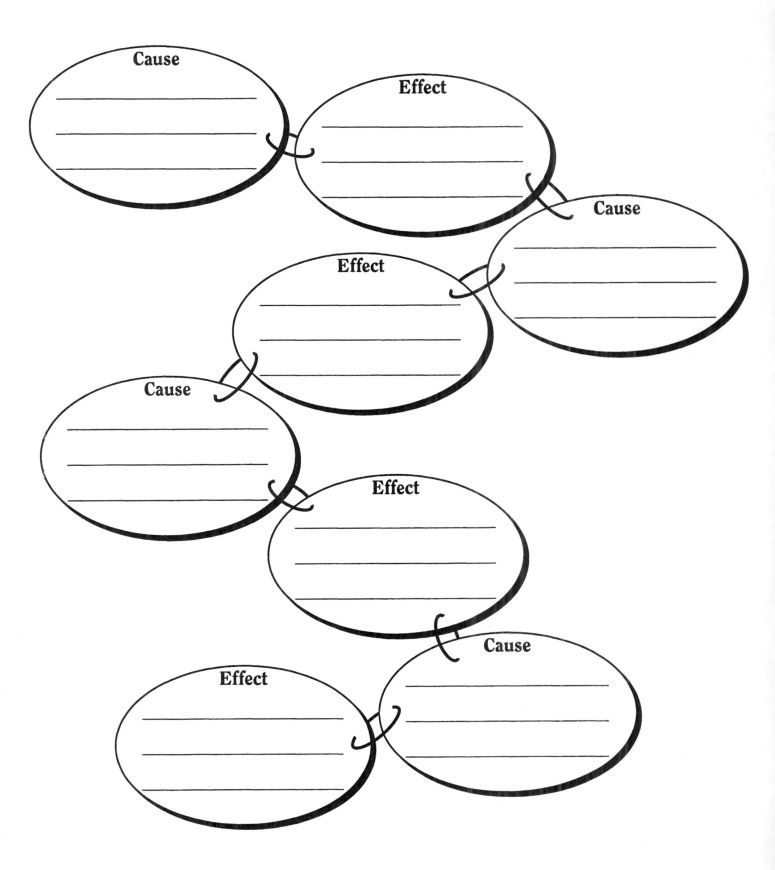

Character Analysis Web

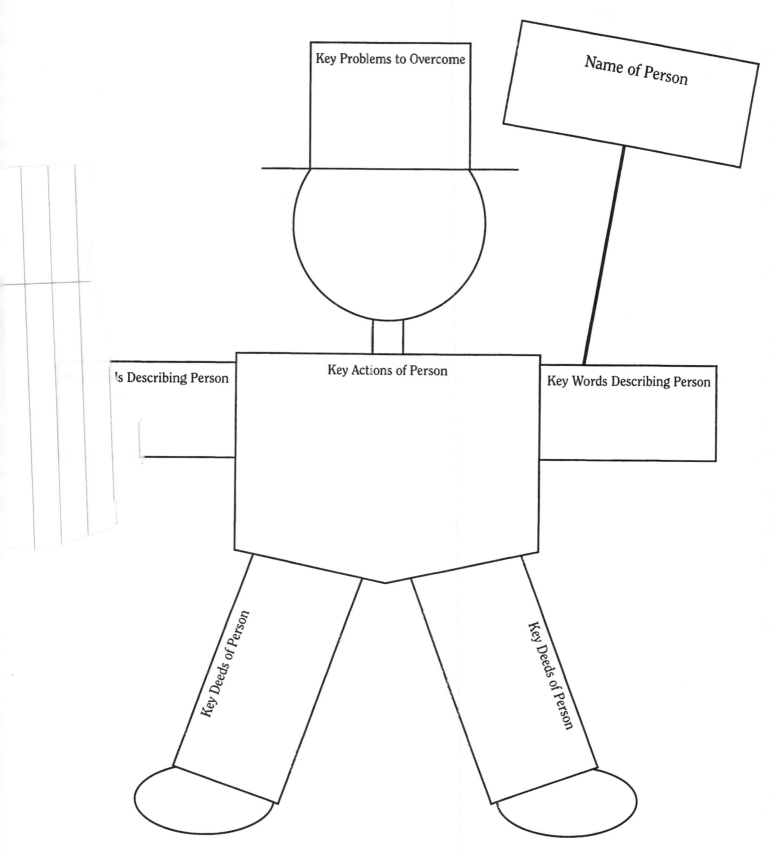

Key Problems to Overcome

Name of Person

Key Actions of Person

ls Describing Person

Key Words Describing Person

Key Deeds of Person

Key Deeds of Person

33

Compare and Contrast

Concept 1 _____

Concept 2 _____

HOW ALIKE?

_____

_____

_____

_____

_____

HOW DIFFERENT?

With Regard To

_____   _____

_____   _____

_____   _____

_____   _____

_____   _____

Standards-Based LANGUAGE ARTS Graphic Organizers, Rubrics, and Writing Prompts for Middle Grade Students

Concept Map

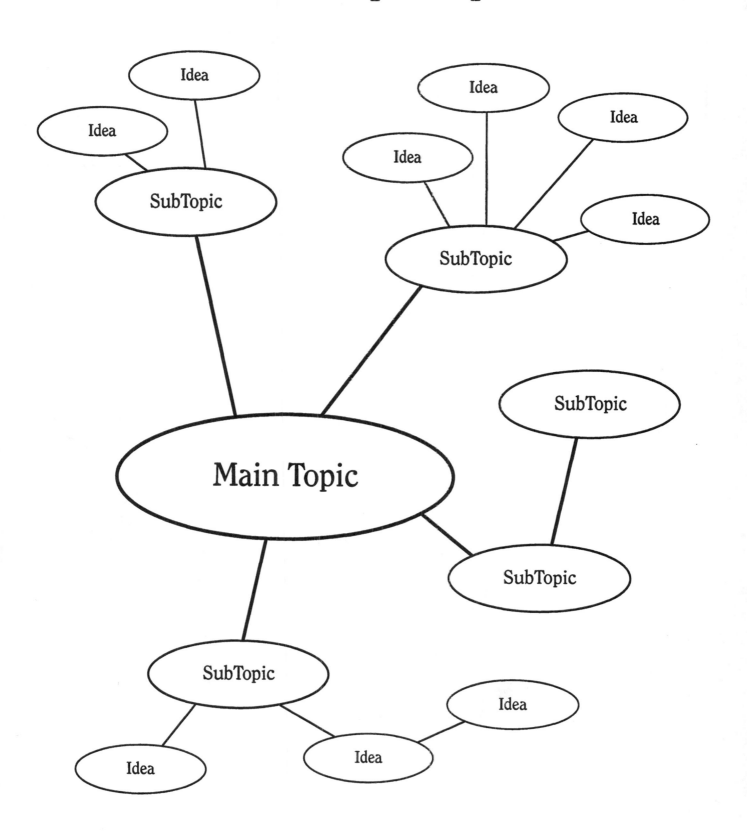

Cycle Organizer

TITLE

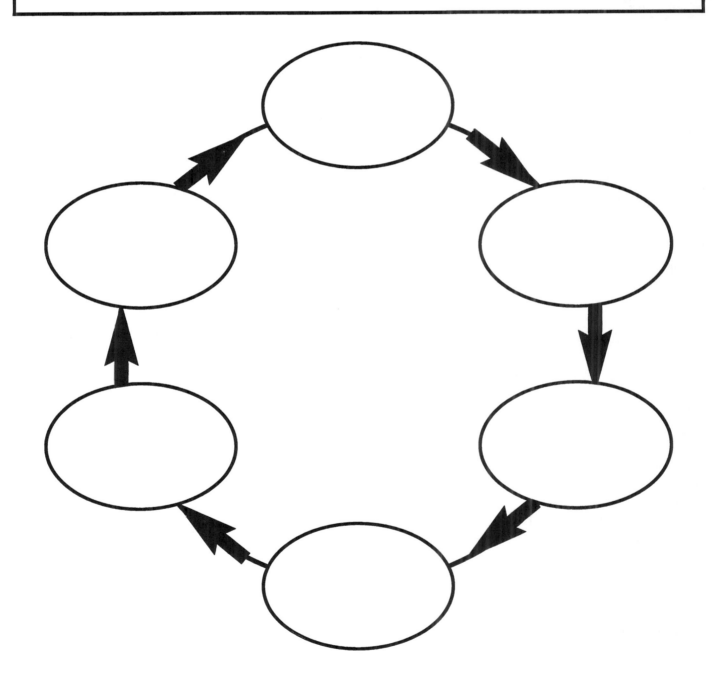

Standards-Based LANGUAGE ARTS Graphic Organizers,
Rubrics, and Writing Prompts for Middle Grade Students

Easy-to-Make Cube Report

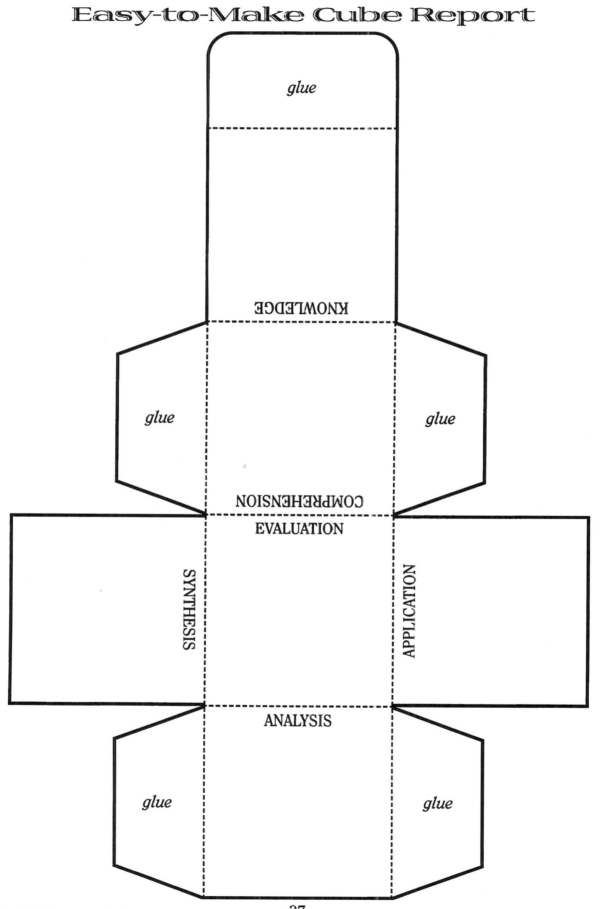

glue

KNOWLEDGE

glue

glue

COMPREHENSION

EVALUATION

SYNTHESIS

APPLICATION

ANALYSIS

glue

glue

Standards-Based LANGUAGE ARTS Graphic Organizers,
Rubrics, and Writing Prompts for Middle Grade Students

Fact and Information Organizer

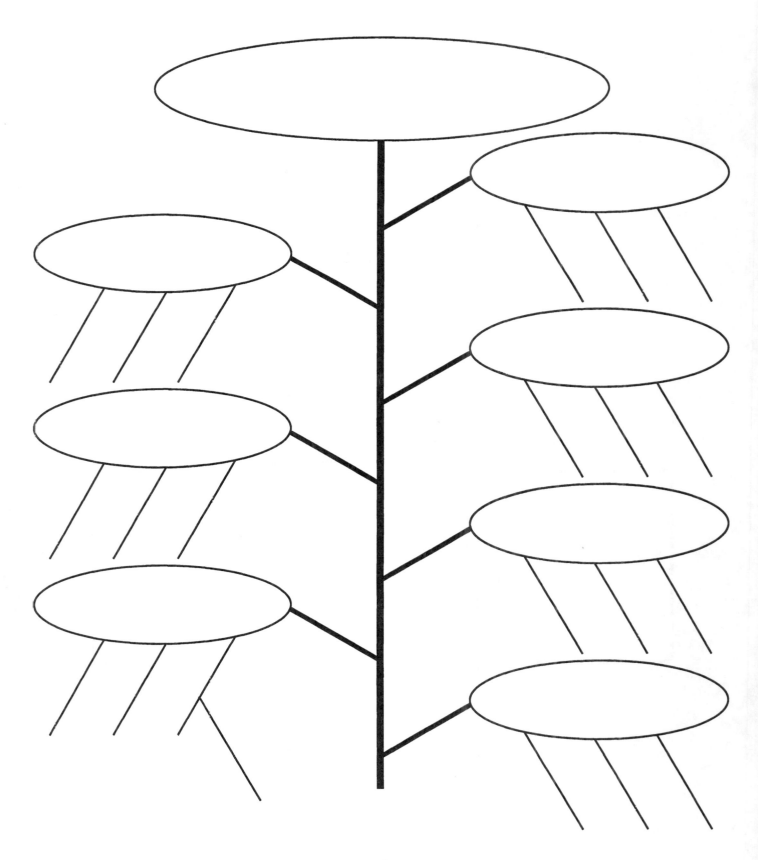

Group Book Report Mural Plan

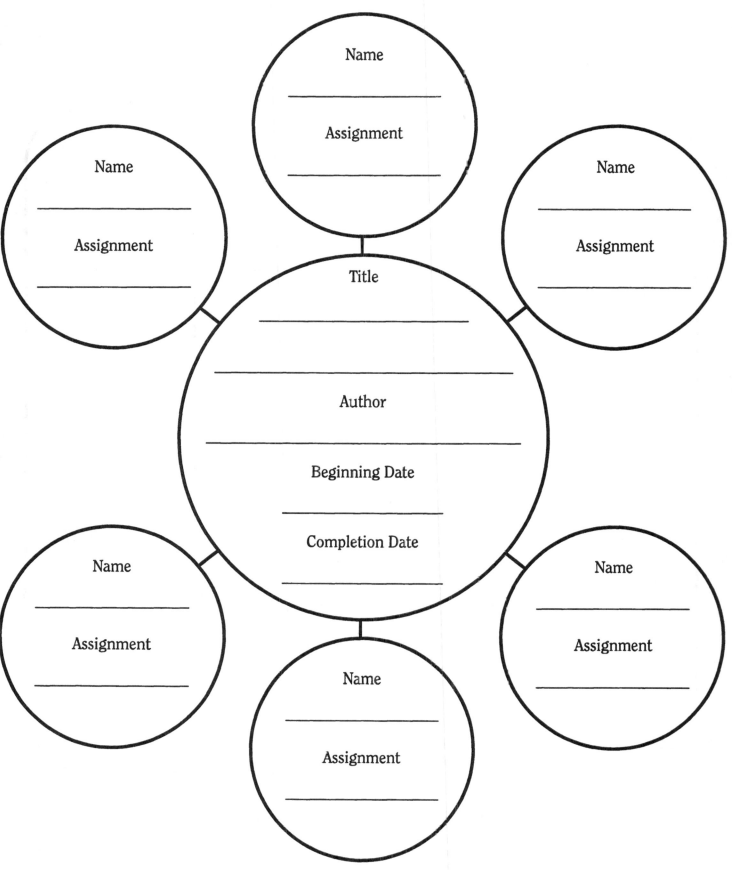

Name

_____

Assignment

_____

Name

_____

Assignment

_____

Name

_____

Assignment

_____

Title

_____

_____

Author

_____

Beginning Date

_____

Completion Date

_____

Name

_____

Assignment

_____

Name

_____

Assignment

_____

Name

_____

Assignment

_____

Standards-Based LANGUAGE ARTS Graphic Organizers,
Rubrics, and Writing Prompts for Middle Grade Students

Independent Project Plan

Topic:_____

Completion Date: _____

Learning Goals:

Materials and
Location:

Project Description:

Plan of Action:

Culmination and
Plan for Sharing with Teacher:

Student Signature: _____ Date: _____

Teacher Signature: _____ Date: _____

Interview Organizer

GETTING READY FOR THE INTERVIEW

Name of Interviewee _____

Name of Interviewer _____

Date of Interview _____

Purpose of Interview _____

_____

CONDUCTING THE INTERVIEW

Question One _____

_____

Response _____

_____

Question Two _____

_____

Response _____

_____

Question Three _____

_____

Response _____

_____

FOLLOWING THE INTERVIEW

Results of Interview _____

_____

_____

_____

_____

Literature Analysis Stairway

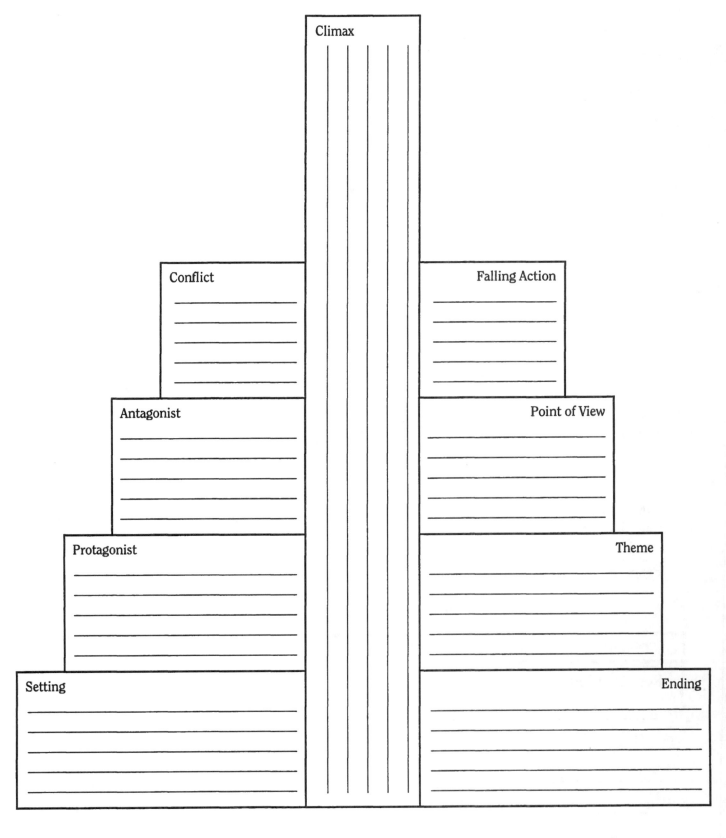

Climax

Conflict

Falling Action

Antagonist

Point of View

Protagonist

Theme

Setting

Ending

Standards-Based LANGUAGE ARTS Graphic Organizers,
Rubrics, and Writing Prompts for Middle Grade Students

Observation Log

Date: _____

Time: _____

Date: _____ Time: _____

Date: _____ Time: _____

Date: _____ Time: _____

Date: _____ Time: _____

Date: _____ Time: _____

Standards-Based LANGUAGE ARTS Graphic Organizers,
Rubrics, and Writing Prompts for Middle Grade Students

Points to Ponder Star

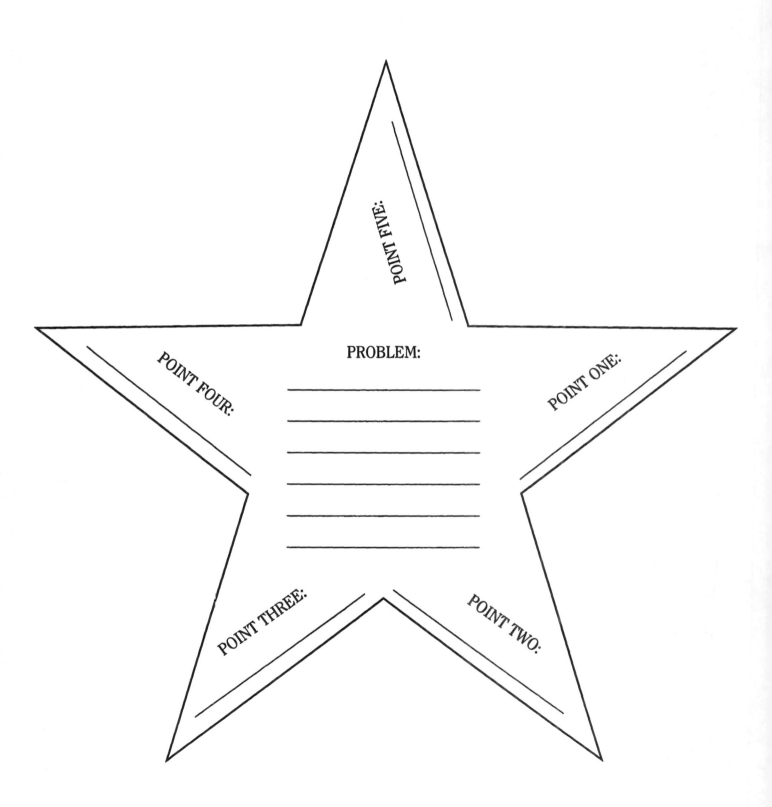

POINT FIVE:

PROBLEM:

POINT FOUR:

POINT ONE:

POINT THREE:

POINT TWO:

Portfolio Planning Guide

Name _____

Title _____

Beginning Date _____ Teacher Approval Date _____

Ending Date _____ Teacher Conference Date _____

Goals and objectives *(what I hope to learn)*

Artifacts to be included

Materials needed

Challenges that may be presented

People and places to use as resources

Questions to find answers for

Method of evaluation

Plan summary and review

Prediction Web

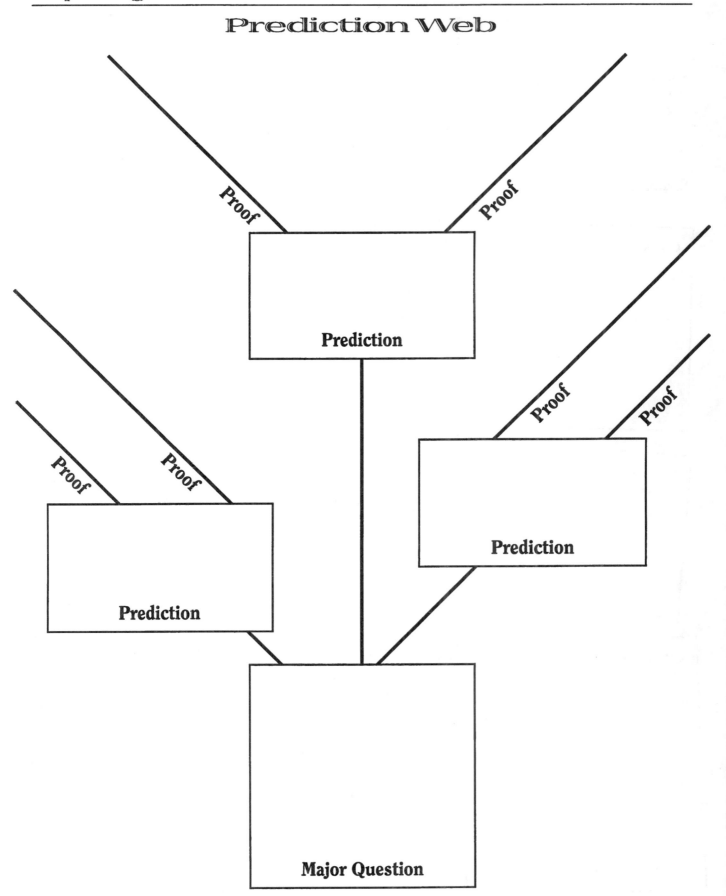

Proof

Proof

Prediction

Proof

Proof

Proof

Proof

Prediction

Prediction

Major Question

Standards-Based LANGUAGE ARTS Graphic Organizers,
Rubrics, and Writing Prompts for Middle Grade Students

Project Tree Planning Tool

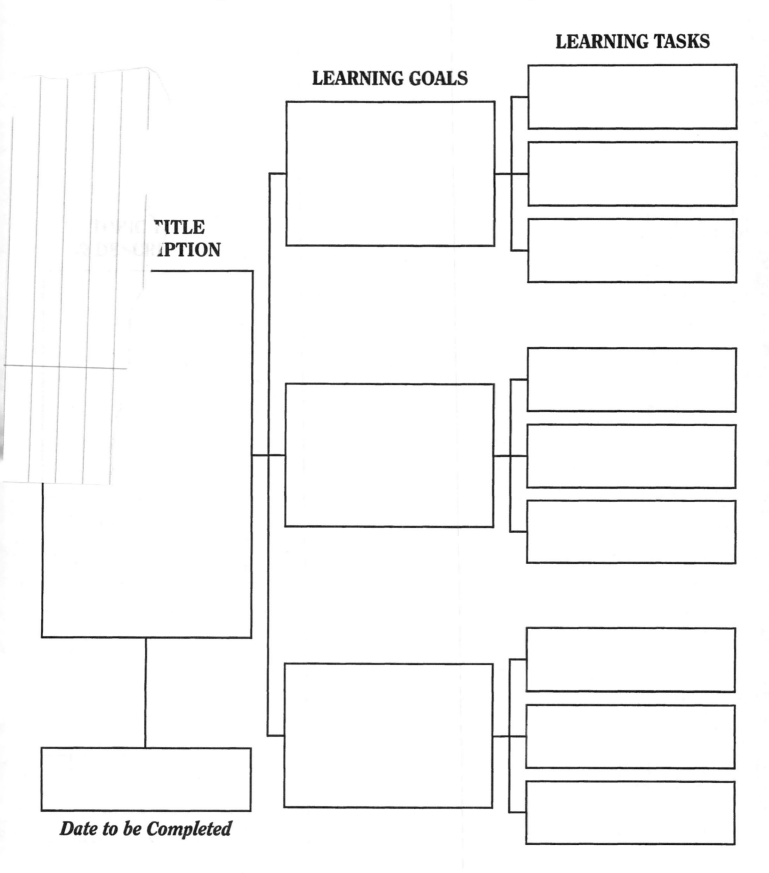

LEARNING TASKS

LEARNING GOALS

TITLE
IPTION

Date to be Completed

*Standards-Based LANGUAGE ARTS Graphic Organizers,
Rubrics, and Writing Prompts for Middle Grade Students*

Puzzle Grid

Title: _____

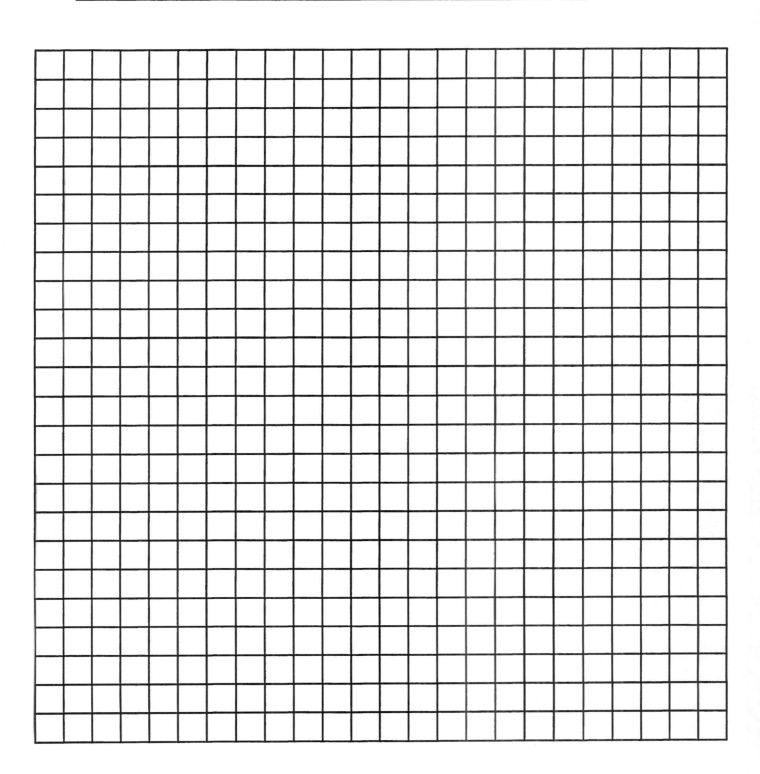

Reporter's Template

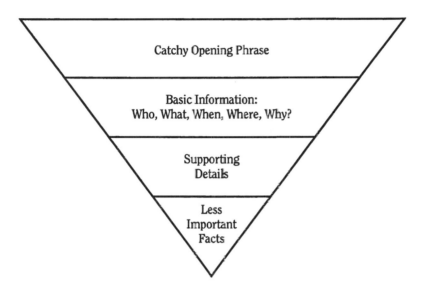

Catchy Opening Phrase: _____

_____

_____

Basic Information: Who, What, When, Where, Why? _____

_____

_____

Supporting Details: _____

_____

_____

Less Important Facts: _____

_____

_____

*Standards-Based LANGUAGE ARTS Graphic Organizers,
Rubrics, and Writing Prompts for Middle Grade Students*

Research Study Plan

PERSONAL PROJECT PLAN

Title and Description of Study	Beginning Date _____ Completion Date _____	Format for Study

Resources Needed and Location

Challenges to be expected and/or questions to answer

Method of Evaluation

Student Signature: _____ Date: _____

Teacher Signature: _____ Date: _____

Scope and Sequence Chart

Historical Setting
Historical Figures
Historical Problem Situation

First Event/Step: _____

Second Event/Step: _____

Third Event/Step: _____

Fourth Event/Step: _____

Fifth Event/Step: _____

Outcomes: _____ _____
Resolution: _____ _____

Standards-Based LANGUAGE ARTS Graphic Organizers,
Rubrics, and Writing Prompts for Middle Grade Students

Story Board

1.

6.

2.

7.

3.

8.

4.

9.

5.

10.

SQ3R Chart

Directions

This chart is helpful when reading a chapter from a textbook. Use one chart for each major section of the chapter. Remember that SQ3R means:

Survey: Read titles/subtitles. Notice words/phrases in special type.
Skim illustrations/charts/graphs. Review end-of-chapter summaries and questions.

Question: Turn main/subtopics in special print into 5W questions—Who, What, When, Where, and Why.

Read: Read information to answer questions, highlighting main ideas and taking notes.

Recite: Pause at the end of each chapter section to answer questions orally, using your own words.

Review: Construct a study guide sheet that includes summaries and main ideas from your reading.

Survey: Record most important titles and subtitles from major chapter section.

_____

_____

_____

_____

Question: Write Who, What, When, Where, and Why questions for main/subtopics.

_____

_____

_____

_____

Read: Write short answers to five questions from above.

_____

_____

_____

_____

Standards-Based LANGUAGE ARTS Graphic Organizers, Rubrics, and Writing Prompts for Middle Grade Students

The 5 Ws and How Web

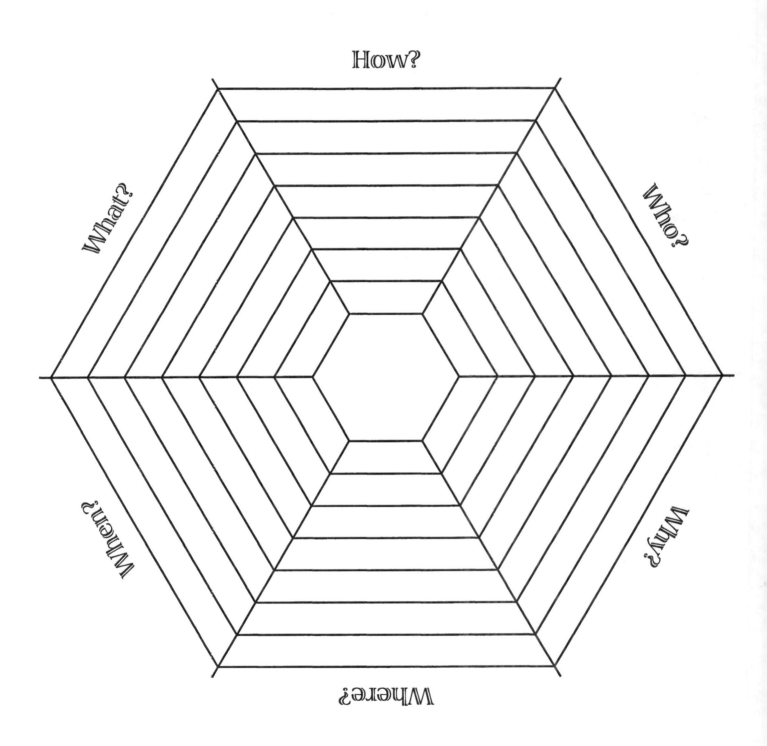

How?

What?

Who?

When?

Where?

Why?

Standards-Based LANGUAGE ARTS Graphic Organizers, Rubrics, and Writing Prompts for Middle Grade Students

Umbrella Organizer

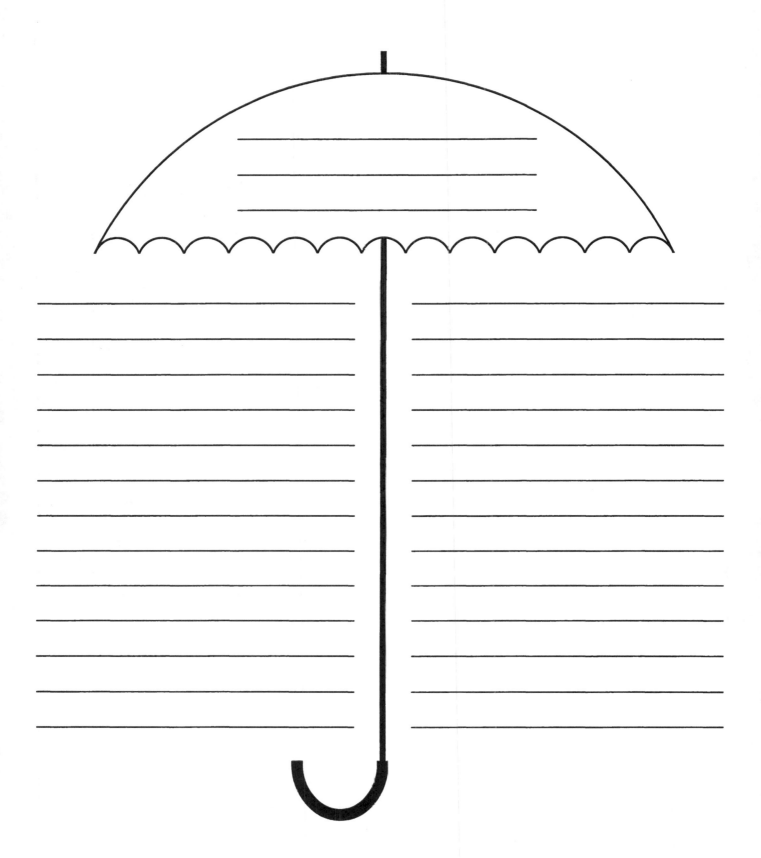

Standards-Based LANGUAGE ARTS Graphic Organizers,
Rubrics, and Writing Prompts for Middle Grade Students

Vocabulary Learning Ladder

Word or Term: _____

Textbook Sentence: _____

Page: _____ Definition: _____

_____

5

Word or Term: _____

Textbook Sentence: _____

Page: _____ Definition: _____

_____

4

Word or Term: _____

Textbook Sentence: _____

Page: _____ Definition: _____

_____

3

Word or Term: _____

Textbook Sentence: _____

Page: _____ Definition: _____

_____

2

Word or Term: _____

Textbook Sentence: _____

Page: _____ Definition: _____

_____

1

What, So What, Now What?

Topic of Study_____

Student's Name _____

What?	So What?	Now What?

Questions for Teachers and Students to Consider About Using Graphic Organizers in the Classroom

1. What is a graphic organizer and what types of graphic organizers are best for my subject area?

2. How can I use graphic organizers to help students collect information, make interpretations, draw conclusions, solve problems, outline plans, and become better reflective thinkers?

3. What graphic organizers can I use that are hierarchical structures with levels and subsets?

4. What graphic organizers can I use that are conceptual structures which take a central idea or concept and branch out from it?

5. What graphic organizers can I use that are sequential structures that focus on the order, chronology, or flow of ideas?

6. What graphic organizers can I use that are cyclical structures, which form a pattern in a circular format?

7. How can I model the use of graphic organizers with my students before introducing them into the instructional process?

8. How can I best model the use of graphic organizers—with a wall chart, an overhead projector, or a drawing on the chalkboard?

9. How do graphic organizers show and explain relationships between content and sub-content and how do they in turn relate to the other content areas?

10. How can graphic organizers be considered teaching tools for all types of learners?

11. How can graphic organizers be used as assessment tools to show a student's understanding of a concept and a student's way of thinking about that concept?

12. How do graphic organizers support Bloom's Taxonomy and the Multiple Intelligences?

13. Are graphic organizers best used with individual students, or can they be part of cooperative learning group tasks?

14. How can students use graphic organizers to assess their own learning?

Standards-Based LANGUAGE ARTS Graphic Organizers, Rubrics, and Writing Prompts for Middle Grade Students

Writing Prompts

Explain *figurative language* and tell why it is important to a poet.

Imagine you are a famous producer of films. You have just been hired to create a documentary on the most unique or unusual culture in the world. What culture would you choose and what would your documentary be like?

Write a condensed version of your autobiography. Be sure to include details to make it as interesting to the reader as possible.

GUIDELINES
For Using Journals

PURPOSE

A journal is: a collection of ideas, thoughts, and opinions; a place to outline papers and projects, a place to record observations about something read, written or discussed, a record keeping tool, a place in which to write personal reactions or responses, a reference file to help a student monitor individual growth, a way for students to dialogue with teachers and peers, a place for a student to write about a variety of topics, and a place for reflections on learned material.

FORMATS

Several formats are available for students working with journal writing. Some of the most appealing formats to students and teachers are: special notebooks, segments of audiotapes, file cards, and handmade diaries.

WRITING TIME

There are several approaches students may use in timing their journal writing. Some may write daily for five minutes, semi-weekly for ten minutes, weekly for fifteen minutes, or as inspiration strikes.

STUDENT FEEDBACK

There are several methods, both formal and informal, for sharing students' journal work. Choose one or more of the following to implement in your classroom.

1) Students share their journal entries with their peers.

2) Students read journal entries aloud to the class on a volunteer basis.

3) Journals may be used for "conferencing."

4) Journals are to be taken home and shared with parents or guardians.

5) Students may analyze and answer one of their own journal entries one or more days after entry was recorded to acknowledge personal changes in perspective.

Standards-Based LANGUAGE ARTS Graphic Organizers, Rubrics, and Writing Prompts for Middle Grade Students

Copyright ©2001 by Incentive Publications, Inc.
Nashville, TN.

21 WRITING PROMPTS

for Anytime Use
to Spark Critical and Creative Thinking

1. Write about what you are doing in class. Consider things that are hard, fun, interesting, confusing, funny, valuable, or challenging. Consider comments about group discussions, homework assignments, independent study options, lectures, or tests/exams.

2. Describe any of the assignments from the teachers using your own words or interpretations.

3. Define specific terms and concepts as you understand or confront them.

4. Compare and contrast two or more assignments, projects, performances, or other learning activities.

5. Explain how to show or perform a specific skill or act.

6. Make realistic guesses about what could have happened if you had done something or some assignment differently.

7. Question what your students are learning or doing using a dialogue format.

8. Plan a project or performance with details and expected outcomes.

9. Evaluate your assigned work in a particular class or course.

10. Compose a reaction to something you studied with which you strongly agree or disagree.

11. Paraphrase or summarize a complex idea so that it makes more sense to you.

12. Disclose a reaction to something about which you feel strongly.

13. Build or develop a model, theory, or idea from scratch.

14. Set up an experiment to test a hypothesis.

15. Draw conclusions from a given set of data.

16. Consider an issue or concept from two or more different perspectives.

17. Determine the worth or value of something learned in class.

18. Create a solution to a specific dilemma or problem or identify the factors or variables that caused a certain decision to be made.

19. Form some generalizations about an assigned topic or problem.

20. Create, compose, design, or develop something new and unique.

21. Complete a series of starter statements such as:
I wonder . . . . I wish . . . . I have learned that . . . . I need help with . . . . If only . . . . I was surprised to find that . . . .

Standards-Based LANGUAGE ARTS Graphic Organizers, Rubrics, and Writing Prompts for Middle Grade Students

Identify a trend that you see becoming popular in your school or community, such as a behavior, a form of dress, a food fad, fondness for a type of entertainment, etc. Make a list of possible effects and influences that may result from this trend. Suggest ways for measuring the growth, development, and consequences of this trend.

_____

_____

_____

_____

_____

_____

_____

_____

Write a reflective essay describing your reading habits, interests, and abilities. Begin by classifying yourself as an avid and enthusiastic reader, a good to average reader, or a reluctant and underachieving reader. List your strengths and weaknesses as a reader and draw on your past experiences to pinpoint some strategies or techniques you might employ to become a better or more proficient reader.

_____

_____

_____

_____

_____

_____

_____

_____

Standards-Based LANGUAGE ARTS Graphic Organizers, Rubrics, and Writing Prompts for Middle Grade Students

The concept of personification is based on giving human-like qualities to inanimate objects or the act of assigning human-like attributes to non-human creatures. Even though this concept is most often associated with poetry, it is widely used in other contexts; one of its chief values is that it draws heavily on the writer's imagination and spurs creative thinking. Select one of the story starters below to write an imaginative story in first person, portraying such things as feelings, actions, beliefs, associates, etc.

1. My life as a red pencil in a language arts teacher's classroom

2. My life as a microphone in a recording studio used by a popular rock and roll group

3. My life as a language arts textbook used by a middle grades student

_____

_____

_____

_____

_____

_____

Create a detailed outline for a series of pantomimes or pageantry scenes to present the actions, emotions, and reactions of a student whose native language is one other than the one used in the classroom in which he or she is a student, in each of the following situations:

1. First visit to the school cafeteria

2. Receiving and being expected to complete a written assignment in a language other than the student's native one

3. Participating in a class discussion using a foreign language

_____

_____

_____

_____

_____

_____

_____

Design a greeting card to send to a family member or to a friend expressing appreciation for something they do on a regular basis to make your life easier or more pleasant. Select a theme for the card and carry it out in both the graphics and written copy. Use your imagination to convey the message in the most personalized and creative manner possible.

_____

_____

_____

_____

_____

_____

_____

_____

_____

_____

Pretend you are a movie or television critic and have been assigned to write a review of a popular movie or TV program with which you are familiar. Write the review with attention to: character, plot, use of time, writing style, delivery of dialogue, props and staging, relevancy of content to topic, interest to audience, and creativity.

_____

_____

_____

_____

_____

_____

_____

_____

_____

_____

Standards-Based LANGUAGE ARTS Graphic Organizers,
Rubrics, and Writing Prompts for Middle Grade Students

Select one of the topics below that you feel strongly for or against to use as the subject of a debate. Prepare detailed notes to support your stand in a class debate. Use reference materials as needed to gain information to support your position.

1. Year-round schooling for all middle grades

2. Mandatory community service for every high school senior

3. Free health care for every citizen, from birth until death

_____

_____

_____

_____

_____

_____

_____

_____

Select a historical, geographical, or political subject that highly interests you. Quickly write a list of ten to twenty things you know about the subject. Use reference materials to check the accuracy of the facts on your list. Mark the factual statements with an *F* and the statements that are not 100% factual with an *O* (for *opinion*).

_____

_____

_____

_____

_____

_____

_____

_____

_____

_____

_____

Standards-Based LANGUAGE ARTS Graphic Organizers,
Rubrics, and Writing Prompts for Middle Grade Students

Design a learning poster to teach someone whose language is different from your own how to complete a simple task associated with the routine of a typical day in your school, such as making use of school lockers, checking out books in the library, accessing and using computers, etc. Remember you will need to rely heavily on graphics and limit your use of words.

_____

_____

_____

_____

_____

_____

_____

_____

_____

_____

In your imagination, invent a brand new product of value to a student your age. Describe the product, its use and purpose, materials and skills necessary for producing it, and how it would be packaged and marketed. Create a package label, a warranty, and a sales promotional piece for the product. Critically read your completed work and answer the big question with one of the following three responses: *yes*   *maybe*   *no*

The big question: **WOULD YOU BUY THIS PRODUCT?**

_____

_____

_____

_____

_____

_____

_____

_____

Standards-Based LANGUAGE ARTS Graphic Organizers,
Rubrics, and Writing Prompts for Middle Grade Students

Draw a scene for a postcard depicting the setting of one of your favorite novels, short stories, or plays. Write a message that one of the characters in the work might send to another one of the characters. Write the message that the recipient of the postmark might create in response.

_____

_____

_____

_____

_____

_____

_____

_____

_____

Create a survey or questionnaire to be used to measure the attitudes, knowledge and/or positions of students, faculty, and administrators in your school related to a controversial issue within the school community. Think through each question carefully and revise it as needed to focus specifically on the issue and to elicit an honest and candid response.

_____

_____

_____

_____

_____

_____

_____

_____

_____

If you had to choose a life career from the following fields, would you: act in movies, serve in public office, travel the world meeting people and writing feature articles for a travel magazine, become an artist, become an author, or become a teacher?

Write a paragraph to share with your classmates, giving reasons for your choice of careers.

_____

_____

_____

_____

_____

_____

_____

_____

_____

Make a list of twenty quality questions you have related to the topic you are currently studying in science or social studies. List at least one source for each question to help you formulate an answer for the question.

_____

_____

_____

_____

_____

_____

_____

_____

_____

_____

Standards-Based LANGUAGE ARTS Graphic Organizers, Rubrics, and Writing Prompts for Middle Grade Students

Copyright ©2001 by Incentive Publications, Inc. Nashville, TN.

Imagine you are a famous producer of films. You have just been hired to create a documentary on the most unique or unusual culture in the world. What culture would you choose and what would your documentary be like?

_____

_____

_____

_____

_____

_____

_____

_____

_____

_____

Describe your favorite Chinese, Mexican, Italian, French, or Turkish food in mouth-watering terms. Use the most figurative language and explicative descriptive words in your vocabulary to portray the color and excitement of the food's origin. Draw a picture to embellish your description.

_____

_____

_____

_____

_____

_____

_____

_____

_____

Standards-Based LANGUAGE ARTS Graphic Organizers,
Rubrics, and Writing Prompts for Middle Grade Students

Write a letter, using friendly letter format, to a person in another country. Tell them about the advantages your state offers as a vacation spot. Then, use the same information to compose an e-mail conveying the same information to the same person.

_____

_____

_____

_____

_____

_____

_____

_____

_____

_____

_____

Write a condensed version of your autobiography. Be sure to include details to make it as interesting to the reader as possible.

_____

_____

_____

_____

_____

_____

_____

_____

_____

_____

_____

_____

Standards-Based LANGUAGE ARTS Graphic Organizers, Rubrics, and Writing Prompts for Middle Grade Students

Copyright ©2001 by Incentive Publications, Inc. Nashville, TN.

Design a comic strip based on an incident from your typical school day. Select characters, design graphics, and write dialogue to entice your reader to be interested in the next episode.

_____

_____

_____

_____

_____

_____

_____

_____

_____

_____

Write a letter to a teacher or a school administrator explaining a problem occurring in your school at the present time. Recommend a remedy for this situation.

_____

_____

_____

_____

_____

_____

_____

_____

_____

_____

*Standards-Based LANGUAGE ARTS Graphic Organizers,
Rubrics, and Writing Prompts for Middle Grade Students*

Compose a letter, using the correct business letter format, to a local, state, or national lawmaker (mayor, legislator, senator, governor, President, etc.) Express your opinion about a piece of pending legislation or a change in the law related to an area concerning your state, county, town, or city.

_____

_____

_____

_____

_____

_____

_____

_____

_____

_____

Use one of the following starters to write a tall tale:

When I looked out the window to see the spaceship landing right in my front yard . . .

The town will never be the same again since . . .

Like a bird in the sky, once the boy's feet left the ground . . .

_____

_____

_____

_____

_____

_____

_____

_____

_____

_____

72

Write an essay for inclusion in a class anthology on one of the following values: honesty, responsibility, loyalty, or respect.

_____
_____
_____
_____
_____
_____
_____
_____
_____
_____
_____

Create a study guide to help you understand and appreciate a Shakespearean play.

_____
_____
_____
_____
_____
_____
_____
_____
_____
_____
_____
_____
_____

Standards-Based LANGUAGE ARTS Graphic Organizers,
Rubrics, and Writing Prompts for Middle Grade Students

Write a letter to your principal or assistant principal expressing your feelings about the school's discipline rules. Be sure to justify your opinions with examples, possible consequences, and other subjective reasoning.

_____
_____
_____
_____
_____
_____
_____
_____
_____
_____

Create a billboard advertisement, a T.V. commercial, a radio announcement, and a newspaper advertisement to promote attendance at an upcoming school carnival whose purpose is to raise funds to purchase computer equipment for your school.

_____
_____
_____
_____
_____
_____
_____
_____
_____
_____

Standards-Based LANGUAGE ARTS Graphic Organizers, Rubrics, and Writing Prompts for Middle Grade Students

Most folklore is derived from stories, fables, and myths that were first told and passed by word of mouth from generation to generation. Many have a moral theme and include a villain and a hero. Some stories chronicle events of the time.

Create a piece of folklore based on some popular cultural phenomenon or life event today that you think would be interesting to people your age 50 years from now.

_____

_____

_____

_____

_____

_____

_____

_____

_____

_____

Step One: Without using any reference materials, write the best one-sentence definition you can for the use of each of the pronunciation marks below. Leave a blank line beneath each definition.

    1. period

    2. exclamation mark

    3. quotation mark

    4. comma

    5. semi-colon

    6. colon

Step Two: On the blank line beneath each definition, write a sentence about something happening this week in your classroom using the punctuation mark defined.

Step Three: If you have doubts about the accuracy of your definitions, use reference materials to modify your sentences if necessary.

Standards-Based LANGUAGE ARTS Graphic Organizers,
Rubrics, and Writing Prompts for Middle Grade Students

Some people feel certain books are inappropriate for inclusion in public library collections. This may be because of the content, the graphics, or, in some instances, both the content and the graphics. Other people feel that the potential reader should have freedom of choice.

What do you think?

I think books . . .

_____

_____

_____

_____

_____

_____

_____

_____

Name your favorite literary genre and explain why you like it.

_____

_____

_____

_____

_____

_____

_____

_____

_____

_____

_____

_____

Standards-Based LANGUAGE ARTS Graphic Organizers, Rubrics, and Writing Prompts for Middle Grade Students

Define a myth, a fairy tale, and a fable. Explain how they are alike and how they are different.

_____

_____

_____

_____

_____

_____

_____

_____

_____

_____

_____

Check one blank below to indicate which method you would prefer to use to study a Shakespearean play. Then write a brief paragraph telling why you chose this method.

_____ Read the play   _____ Watch the movie   _____ Attend the live performance

_____

_____

_____

_____

_____

_____

_____

_____

_____

Standards-Based LANGUAGE ARTS Graphic Organizers,
Rubrics, and Writing Prompts for Middle Grade Students

Circle the descriptive words in each of the three sentences below. Then change the meaning of each sentence entirely by substituting for each circled word a word with an opposite meaning.

- That exotic young lady's consistent exuberance is invigorating and infectious, as is her enthusiasm for life.

- The forbidding beast with bloodthirsty eyes roared ferociously down the narrow, winding road toward its unsuspecting victim.

- The bewildered child huddled forlornly in the center of the busy intersection, unaware of the cold, pelting rain, dark sky, and heavy traffic zooming by on either side of her.

_____

_____

_____

_____

_____

_____

Write a paragraph or a journal entry explaining how you use computers and/ or computer-generated data to communicate with people outside your own community.

_____

_____

_____

_____

_____

_____

_____

_____

_____

_____

_____

Standards-Based LANGUAGE ARTS Graphic Organizers, Rubrics, and Writing Prompts for Middle Grade Students

Write a metaphor to complete each of the statements below.

Music is . . .

Sunsets are . . .

Education is . . .

_____

_____

_____

_____

_____

_____

_____

_____

Explain *figurative language* and explain why it is important to a poet.

_____

_____

_____

_____

_____

_____

_____

_____

_____

_____

_____

Standards-Based LANGUAGE ARTS Graphic Organizers,
Rubrics, and Writing Prompts for Middle Grade Students

Do you think computers will eventually replace books for leisure reading?
Write a paragraph to support your answer.

_____

_____

_____

_____

_____

_____

_____

_____

_____

_____

_____

Complete the following sentences and select one to use as a story starter.

• The best novel I have ever read is . . .

• When the teacher says write about anything you want to, I immediately . . .

• E-mail is gradually replacing many letters . . .

_____

_____

_____

_____

_____

_____

_____

_____

_____

Standards-Based LANGUAGE ARTS Graphic Organizers,
Rubrics, and Writing Prompts for Middle Grade Students

Copyright ©2001 by Incentive Publications, Inc.
Nashville, TN.

Complete the similes below, then write 5 additional similes inspired by some of the most interesting words you can think of (use your dictionary if necessary):

- as complete as _____

- as condescending as _____

- as opaque as _____

- as morose as _____

- as quintessential as _____

_____

_____

_____

_____

_____

_____

_____

Write a letter to the editor of your local newspaper expressing your understanding of and your opinion about the availability of inappropriate programming on the Internet, the influences of these programs on the social and moral values of people your age, and some measures that might be taken to change this situation.

_____

_____

_____

_____

_____

_____

_____

_____

_____

_____

_____

Standards-Based LANGUAGE ARTS Graphic Organizers,
Rubrics, and Writing Prompts for Middle Grade Students

Plan and carry out a virtual field trip via the Internet to a well-known art museum of your choice. Write a detailed report of your visit and critique the works you saw there.

_____

_____

_____

_____

_____

_____

_____

_____

_____

_____

_____

Outline plans for a research project on a topic of high interest to you. List at least three major sources you will use to gather information related to the topic. Make a list of questions you want to find answers for, and develop a time and work plan for doing the research and organizing your research findings to provide a summary report.

_____

_____

_____

_____

_____

_____

_____

_____

_____

_____

_____

Standards-Based LANGUAGE ARTS Graphic Organizers,
Rubrics, and Writing Prompts for Middle Grade Students

Make a list of questions you would like to ask someone you know whose native language is different from your own. Ask the person about daily life and culture in his or her native country. Then make a list of questions you think they might want to ask you about your own daily life. If possible, arrange a discussion period with that person and use your questions as a guide.

_____

_____

_____

_____

_____

_____

_____

_____

Thumb through your social studies or science book for the purpose of evaluating its usability for its intended purpose. Consider the readability of the text, the book's format and organization, the quality of graphics, vocabulary use, interest level of the materials and ease or difficulty of access to factual information. Write a critique of the book; try to be as objective as possible. Compare your critique with one written by a classmate.

_____

_____

_____

_____

_____

_____

_____

_____

Prepare an outline for a speech to be delivered to members of your class stressing the importance of a well-planned character education program for students of your age. Rank order the importance of inclusion of the following values in the program: love, honesty, respect and responsibility. Give reasons for your ranking:

_____

_____

_____

_____

_____

_____

_____

_____

_____

_____

Make a checkmark beside each form of literature below that you have read in the past month. Write a paragraph telling which genre is your favorite for free reading time and why you prefer it.

___ Biography   ___ Poetry   ___ Science Fiction   ___ Folklore

___ Informational   ___ Historical Fiction   ___ Realistic Fiction   ___ Modern Fantasy

_____

_____

_____

_____

_____

_____

_____

_____

Standards-Based LANGUAGE ARTS Graphic Organizers, Rubrics, and Writing Prompts for Middle Grade Students

Copyright ©2001 by Incentive Publications, Inc. Nashville, TN.

Make a list of six sources of information that you could turn to for information on a subject of importance to you right now. Rank order your list in terms of usefulness. Make a star beside each one you have used within the past 60 days.

_____

_____

_____

_____

_____

_____

_____

_____

_____

_____

Write a letter to a student your age living in another country describing your academic goals for the year and telling how you plan to go about achieving them. Include information about the courses you are taking, your access to technology and other resources, and where and how you plan to secure support for your efforts. Ask questions to encourage the recipient of your letter to reply with similar information. You may be surprised by how much you learn about yourself by re-reading your letter.

_____

_____

_____

_____

_____

_____

_____

_____

*Standards-Based LANGUAGE ARTS Graphic Organizers,
Rubrics, and Writing Prompts for Middle Grade Students*

Springboards to Encourage the Use of Thinking and Writing Investigations

Directions

It is important that any project you undertake is manageable in terms of time, energy, resources, and information to be presented. For this reason, you should limit the number of big questions to answer, big ideas to research, or big objectives to cover.

One way to do this is to choose a key behavior, or verb, as the basis for your project. It is important, however, to be wise and cautious as you select the words to define what you will be doing or making.

Some sample springboards are listed below. Use the examples as future project ideas, or refer to them as models for developing your own unique springboards.

1. Compare and contrast _____ with _____ , discussing their similarities and differences.

   _____

   _____

   _____

2. Define and explain the relationship between _____ and _____ .

   _____

   _____

   _____

3. Develop a reasonable hypothesis about something. Then devise a test, experiment, or survey to prove or disprove your hypothesis.

   _____

   _____

   _____

4. Construct a model to appraise something. Label the parts, and create a diagram to show how it works.

   _____

   _____

   _____

Standards-Based LANGUAGE ARTS Graphic Organizers, Rubrics, and Writing Prompts for Middle Grade Students

5. Create a survey or questionnaire to measure outside attitudes, positions, knowledge, or sentiments about a controversial issue. Interpret and publish the results.

_____

_____

_____

6. Observe some people, places, or things. Record what you see. Make inferences or draw conclusions about your observations.

_____

_____

_____

7. Combine two or more ideas/elements/concepts to make a new one.

_____

_____

_____

8. Develop your own theory or philosophy about something.

_____

_____

_____

9. Perform a controlled experiment. Summarize the results and make predictions about future results.

_____

_____

_____

10. Develop a classification scheme. Divide things into categories. Determine appropriate divisions and descriptive labels.

_____

_____

_____

1. How can I fit journals into my particular discipline and classroom schedule?

2. How do I know if journals will work with my students or my subject area?

3. How can I coordinate journals with my team members and their classes?

4. What materials will I need to begin the use of journals?

5. How will I introduce the concept of journals to my students?

6. What kinds of reactions and responses can I expect from my students in their journal entries?

7. How can I get a sense of ownership or interest by students with journal prompts in my classroom?

8. How will I find time to reply to their journals, and what kind of responses should I write?

9. How can I overcome student resistance or misunderstanding of the journal concept?

10. How can I use journals for assessment purposes, and what kinds of information am I likely to receive from them?

11. How should I review or evaluate journals, and how will I keep track of this process?

12. How do I grade journal entries?

Rubrics

Rubric

Cube Report Assessment

Directions: Shade the appropriate number of stars.

Rating Scale: ★★★ Good ★★★ Acceptable ★★ Fine ☆ Needs Work

1. Quality of Report Format
Cube has information relevant to the topic neatly written on all six sides. ☆ ☆ ☆

2. Selection of Information
Important information is carefully selected, and is clearly and concisely reported. ☆ ☆ ☆

3. Grammar
The grammar and spelling of the cube report were carefully checked to avoid misuse or mistakes.

4. Interest
The cube is an attractive and interesting and descriptions important to the

5. Graphics/Creativity
The cube is well-organized in and is neatly put together.

Comments by Student: _____

Signed _____

Comments by Teacher: _____

Signed _____

Overall Rating _____

Signed _____

Rubric

Editor's Final Check

Rating Scale: Good = ✓+   Acceptable = ✓   Needs Work = ✓−

1. Have I visualized my reader? Do I understand what interests his or her? ✓+ ✓ ✓−

2. Have I given careful attention to grammar, spelling, and punctuation so that my reader will experience no confusion in trying to understand my message? (*Proofread your writing, then have a person skilled in proofreading recheck for technical errors.*) ✓+ ✓ ✓−

3. Have I expressed my thought in logical, sequential order? (*Number the main ideas to check this.*) ✓+ ✓ ✓−

4. Have I used plain, simple words in ways with which my reader will be comfortable? ✓+ ✓ ✓−

5. Have I used these plain, simple words in ways that will interest my reader? ✓+ ✓ ✓−

6. Have I deleted unnecessary words or phrases?

7. Have I deleted unrelated or irrelevant matter? (*Underline sentences or phrases that may not relate*)

8. Have I omitted any vital or important details or info

9. Have I avoided overworked words, phrases, and cliché

10. Have I used the most active and interesting words (*Look at each adjective and adverb. Ask yourself i interesting, more picturesque, or more precise wo*)

11. Have I used illustrations or examples to reinforce (*Make an X at places where such entries may be*)

12. Have I created added interest by interspersing fig forceful repetition, or exclamations into ordinary (*Count the number of question marks, exclamati quotation marks, and figures of speech you have*)

13. Have I expressed what I honestly feel or believe, more concerned about what my teacher or my pe (*Use tact and sensitivity when expressing nega feelings or ideas, but do not sacrifice clarity or*)

14. Is my writing clear, neat, and easy to read?

15. Have I referred to the introduction in the conclu and left my reader with an idea to ponder? Have I said anything to cause my reader to rec

100

Rubric

The Graphic Organizer Report Assessment

Rating Scale: = High flyer = Airborne = Grounded

1. Quality of Report Format:
The graphic organizer selected is an appropriate choice for use in the report. Rating: _____

2. Quality of Information:
The information shows significant research on the topic. Rating: _____

3. Grammar:
Spelling, grammar, and punctuation have been carefully checked. Rating: _____

4. Interest:
The different subtopics fit together well and highlight the main points of the topic. Rating: _____

5. Graphics/Creativity:
The graphic organizer fits the information to be organized and is used in a unique and/or creative way to convey the information as efficiently as possible. Rating: _____

Comments by Student: _____

Signed _____ Date _____

Comments by Teacher: _____

Signed _____ Date _____

Overall Rating: _____

Signed _____ Date _____

101

Guidelines
For Using Rubrics

1. Agree on a definition of a rubric and its importance to the evaluation process. The purpose of a rubric is to answer the question: "What are the conditions of success and to what degree are those conditions met by the student involved in a specific learning task?"

2. Effective rubrics reflect the most important elements of an assigned task, product, or performance and they enable both student and teacher to accurately depict the level of competence or stage of development of that student.

3. Effective rubrics encourage student self-evaluations and, in fact, are shared with students prior to beginning the task so that students know exactly what represents quality work.

4. Rubrics are designed to explain more concretely what a child knows and can do and are less subjective than other means of student evaluation.

5. Every rubric must have two components, which are: (1) characteristics or criteria for quality work on a specific task, and (2) determination of the specific levels of proficiency or degrees of success for each part of a task.

6. A holistic rubric consists of paragraphs arranged in a hierarchy so that each level of proficiency has a paragraph describing factors that would result in that specific level.

7. An analytic rubric consists of a listing of criteria most characteristic of that task accompanied with the degrees of success for each model listed separately beside or under each criterion.

8. Before implementing rubrics in a discipline, it is important to define and discuss the elements of a quality performance in that discipline and to collect samples of rubrics as models for scrutiny and potential application.

Standards-Based LANGUAGE ARTS Graphic Organizers,
Rubrics, and Writing Prompts for Middle Grade Students

9. Before implementing rubrics in a discipline, study samples of student work to determine realistic attributes common to varied performances at different levels of proficiency. Translate these attributes into descriptors for the degrees of proficiency and then establish a rating scale to delineate those degrees of proficiency.

10. Avoid using generalities such as *good, better, little, none,* or *somewhat* in your rating scales; quantify and qualify in more specific terms. Construct analytical rubrics with four to six degrees of proficiency for each criterion. Then, weight each criterion to determine the percentage or number of points each is worth.

11. Distribute and discuss any rubric directly with the student before he or she embarks on the assigned product or performance task. Encourage the student to set personal goals for their desired level of accomplishment on each criterion. Insist that students revise their work if it does not meet minimum expectations on any criterion of the task.

12. When introducing rubrics to students, start out by collaboratively constructing a rubric for a fun class event such as planning a party, structuring a field trip, or designing a contest.

13. Remember that to be most effective as an important component of language arts programs, rubrics must be accompanied by carefully planned opportunities for meta-cognitive reflections throughout the assessment experience. While rubrics are comprised of checklists containing sets of criteria for measuring the elements of product, performance, or portfolio, the meta-cognitive reflections provide for self-assessment observations completely unique to the students' own learning goals, expectations, and experiences.

14. The use of rubrics can augment, reinforce, personalize, and strengthen but not replace the assessment program mandated by curriculum guidelines or system requirements. As with any well-balanced assessment program the master teacher or teaching team will continue to take full advantage of all tools, strategies, and techniques available to construct and make use of a balanced assessment program to meet individual needs.

Rubric

Book-Sharing Group Performance

Title of Book _____

Author _____

Publisher _____ Copyright Date _____

Group Members: _____

_____

Rating Scale: Shade in the number of blocks to show your rating

☐ ☐ ☐ = Very Good   ☐ ☐ = Good   ☐ = Not so Good

1. Each member of our group completed the reading assignment on time.	☐ ☐ ☐
2. Each member of our group handled his or her group role.	☐ ☐ ☐
3. Each member of our group took turns listening to one another's ideas.	☐ ☐ ☐
4. Each member of our group was actively engaged in the assigned learning task.	☐ ☐ ☐
5. Each member of our group applied his or her conflict resolution skills when appropriate to do so.	☐ ☐ ☐
6. Each member of our group showed respect for one another.	☐ ☐ ☐
7. Each member of our group made a major contribution to the overall performance.	☐ ☐ ☐
8. Each member of our group displayed a sense of humor.	☐ ☐ ☐
9. Each member of our group contributed original and creative ideas to the discussion.	☐ ☐ ☐
10. Each member of our group participated in the evaluation and assessment of the performance results.	☐ ☐ ☐

Summary: If I were the teacher and the audience of this performance, I would rate our group's

performance as _____ for the following three reasons:

1. _____

2. _____

3. _____

Name _____ Date _____

Brochure Assessment

Rating Scale: Bull's Eye   Good Shot   On Target

1. Brochure Format

Cover, title page, paired pages with paragraphs of information on my subject, and outline drawings are all present when appropriate.

On Target	Bull's Eye
Good Shot	

2. Information

The information in my brochure is carefully researched and accurately presented to give a true account of my subject.

On Target	Bull's Eye
Good Shot	

3. Brochure Organization

My brochure presents information in a logical sequence of paragraphs, giving a comprehensive overview of the subject.

On Target	Bull's Eye
Good Shot	

4. Interest

My brochure uses descriptive words and phrases and is interesting to read.

On Target	Bull's Eye
Good Shot	

5. Grammar

My brochure is written with no grammar or spelling errors.

On Target	Bull's Eye
Good Shot	

6. Graphics/Creativity

The arrangement of and illustrations in my brochure are well done to capture and hold the reader's attention.

On Target	Bull's Eye
Good Shot	

Comments by Student: _____

_____

_____

Signed _____ Date _____

Comments by Teacher: _____

_____

_____

Signed _____ Date _____

Standards-Based LANGUAGE ARTS Graphic Organizers, Rubrics, and Writing Prompts for Middle Grade Students

Chalk Talk Report Assessment

Very good = √ +   Acceptable = √   Needs Work = √ −

	√ +	√	√ −
1. REPORT FORMAT My chalk talk is a brief oral presentation based on a storyboard with numbered frames, illustrations, and explanations of my topic.			
2. INFORMATION The data in my chalk talk is well-researched, and the scope and sequence are presented in a logical order.			
3. GRAMMAR My storyboard and chalk talk contain no grammar, spelling, or punctuation errors.			
4. INTEREST My chalk talk and storyboard make my topic easier to understand and interesting to learn about.			
5. ORGANIZATION My story board is constructed so that I can finish my oral delivery of content and the last details of the visual scenario at the same time.			
6. GRAPHICS/CREATIVITY My chalk talk and story board use visuals and graphics creatively and effectively.			

Student/Teacher Conference Checklist

	Student	Teacher
1. Thorough Research		
2. Organization		
3. Attractive Presentation		
4. Audience Interest		
5. Creativity		
6. Met all requirements of project		
7. Evidence of effort		
8. Overall Rating		

Standards-Based LANGUAGE ARTS Graphic Organizers, Rubrics, and Writing Prompts for Middle Grade Students

Comic Strip Report Assessment

Rating Scale: WOW = 🙂   O.K. = 😐   Boo Hoo = ☹️

1. Quality of Report Format
Comic report is in 8 sections (the first section with the title
and description of report). Relevant cartoon character reports
information on topic with graphics, balloons, etc.   ◯

2. Quality of Information
Relevant and key information is clearly conveyed in a logical sequence.   ◯

3. Grammar
Comic strip is without grammar or spelling errors.   ◯

4. Interest
The comic strip report is interesting and engaging.   ◯

5. Humor
Humor is employed in both language and graphics
to capture and hold the reader's attention.   ◯

6. Graphics/Creativity
Comic includes colorful and creative graphics and drawings.   ◯

Comments by Student: _____

_____

_____

_____

Signed _____ Date _____

Comments by Teacher: _____

_____

_____

_____

Signed _____ Date _____

Content-Based Report Assessment

Rating Scale: Poor Fair Good Great

---

1. Quality of Report Format Rating: _____

The report presents information relevant to the topic with the main points highlighted and explained.

---

2. Selection of Information Rating: _____

Important information is carefully selected from a variety of sources, and is clearly and concisely reported.

---

3. Quality of Resources Rating: _____

The information used is carefully documented, and all sources are accurately given.

---

4. Details and Descriptions Rating: _____

The report is attractive and interesting, and is presented to include details and descriptions important to the topic.

---

5. Grammar Rating: _____

The grammar, punctuation, and spelling of the report were carefully checked to avoid misuse or mistakes.

---

6. Graphics/Creativity Rating: _____

The report is well-organized in an original and creative manner, and is neatly assembled.

Comments by Student: _____

_____

_____

_____

Signed _____ Date _____

Comments by Teacher: _____

_____

_____

_____

Signed _____ Date _____

Cube Report Assessment

Directions: Shade the appropriate number of stars.

Rating Scale: ☆ ☆ ☆ ☆   ☆ ☆ ☆   ☆ ☆   ☆
                  Good   Acceptable   Fine   Needs Work

1. Quality of Report Format   ☆ ☆ ☆ ☆

Cube has information relevant to the topic
neatly written on all six sides.

2. Selection of Information   ☆ ☆ ☆ ☆

Important information is carefully selected,
and is clearly and concisely reported.

3. Grammar   ☆ ☆ ☆ ☆

The grammar and spelling of the cube report
were carefully checked to avoid misuse or mistakes.

4. Interest   ☆ ☆ ☆ ☆

The cube is an attractive and interesting presentation of details
and descriptions important to the topic.

5. Graphics/Creativity   ☆ ☆ ☆ ☆

The cube is well-organized in an original and creative manner,
and is neatly put together.

Comments by Student: _____

_____

_____

Signed _____ Date _____

Comments by Teacher: _____

_____

_____

Signed _____ Date _____

Overall Rating: _____

Signed _____ Date _____

*Standards-Based LANGUAGE ARTS Graphic Organizers,
Rubrics, and Writing Prompts for Middle Grade Students*

Diorama Report Assessment

Rating Scale:

First Place = Excellent	Second Place = Good	Third Place = Fair	Fourth Place = Poor

---

1. Quality of Format

Rating: _____

The diorama conveys information on my topic
in an interesting and thought-provoking manner.

---

2. Quality of Information

Rating: _____

My topic was well-researched, and the diorama conveys
a large amount of correct information that is important to the subject.

---

3. Vocabulary

Rating: _____

The vocabulary utilized for headings or descriptive materials
is carefully selected and properly used to provoke and maintain
an interest and to convey important information.

---

4. Interest

Rating: _____

The diorama is attractive, engaging, and entertaining.

---

5. Graphics/Creativity

Rating: _____

The graphics, images, design, use of color, and layout of my diorama are of high quality.

Comments by Student: _____

_____

_____

_____

Signed _____ Date _____

Comments by Teacher: _____

_____

_____

_____

Signed _____ Date _____

Standards-Based LANGUAGE ARTS Graphic Organizers, Rubrics, and Writing Prompts for Middle Grade Students

Discussion Participation

Rating Scale: Excellent = ! ! !   Good = ! !   Fair = !

1. My participation in the discussion was cheerful,
   enthusiastic, and supportive of the other group members.   **Rating:** _____

2. I contributed ideas and/or information
   to the discussion.   **Rating:** _____

3. My contributions were well-thought out
   and carefully phrased.   **Rating:** _____

4. I listened attentively and appreciatively to the ideas
   and opinions expressed by other group members.   **Rating:** _____

5. When a group member expressed ideas or opinions
   that were not in agreement with my own, I accepted
   them courteously and with an open mind.   **Rating:** _____

6. I kept the subject of the discussion in mind
   at all times and refrained from comments
   not pertinent to the topic under discussion.   **Rating:** _____

7. I gained new and/or different insights
   or information from the discussion.   **Rating:** _____

Comments by Student: _____

_____

_____

_____

Signed _____ Date _____

Comments by Teacher: _____

_____

_____

_____

Signed _____ Date _____

*Standards-Based LANGUAGE ARTS Graphic Organizers,
Rubrics, and Writing Prompts for Middle Grade Students*

Editor's Final Check

Rating Scale: Good = √+   Acceptable = √   Needs Work = √−

1. Have I visualized my reader? Do I understand what interests him or her?	√+ √ √−
2. Have I given careful attention to grammar, spelling, and punctuation so that my reader will experience no confusion in trying to understand my message? *(Proofread your writing, then have a person skilled in proofreading recheck for technical errors.)*	√+ √ √−
3. Have I expressed my thought in logical, sequential order? *(Number the main ideas to check this.)*	√+ √ √−
4. Have I used plain, simple words in ways with which my reader will be comfortable?	√+ √ √−
5. Have I used these plain, simple words in ways that will interest my reader?	√+ √ √−
6. Have I deleted unnecessary words or phrases?	√+ √ √−
7. Have I deleted unrelated or irrelevant matter? *(Underline sentences or phrases that may not relate.)*	√+ √ √−
8. Have I omitted any vital or important details or information?	√+ √ √−
9. Have I avoided overworked words, phrases, and cliches?	√+ √ √−
10. Have I used the most active and interesting words possible to express my ideas? *(Look at each adjective and adverb. Ask yourself if there is a better, more interesting, more picturesque, or more precise word you might substitute.)*	√+ √ √−
11. Have I used illustrations or examples to reinforce main ideas? *(Make an X at places where such entries may be helpful.)*	√+ √ √−
12. Have I created added interest by interspersing figures of speech, forceful repetition, or exclamations into ordinary declarative thought? *(Count the number of question marks, exclamation points, quotation marks, and figures of speech you have used.)*	√+ √ √−
13. Have I expressed what I honestly feel or believe, or have I been more concerned about what my teacher or my peers will think? *(Use tact and sensitivity when expressing negative or unpopular feelings or ideas, but do not sacrifice clarity or effectiveness.)*	√+ √ √−
14. Is my writing clear, neat, and easy to read?	√+ √ √−
15. Have I referred to the introduction in the conclusion and left my reader with an idea to ponder? Have I said anything to cause my reader to reconsider the subject?	√+ √ √−

The Graphic Organizer Report Assessment

Rating Scale: = High flyer  = Airborne  = Grounded

1. **Quality of Report Format:** The graphic organizer selected is an appropriate choice for use in the report.	Rating: _____
2. **Quality of Information:** The information shows significant research on the topic.	Rating: _____
3. **Grammar:** Spelling, grammar, and punctuation have been carefully checked.	Rating: _____
4. **Interest:** The different subtopics fit together well and highlight the main points of the topic.	Rating: _____
5. **Graphics/Creativity:** The graphic organizer fits the information to be organized and is used in a unique and/or creative way to convey the information as efficiently as possible.	Rating: _____

Comments by Student: _____

_____

_____

_____

Signed _____ Date _____

Comments by Teacher: _____

_____

_____

_____

Signed _____ Date _____

Overall Rating: _____

Signed _____ Date _____

Standards-Based LANGUAGE ARTS Graphic Organizers, Rubrics, and Writing Prompts for Middle Grade Students

Group Book Report Mural Assessment

Name:_____

Topic: _____

Overall Theme of Mural: _____

Assigned Topic for Mural: _____

Ideas for My Mural Section: _____

_____

_____

_____

_____

_____

_____

Group Book Report Mural Plan:

Name _____
Assignment _____

Name _____
Assignment _____

Name _____
Assignment _____

Title _____
Author _____
Beginning Date _____
Completion Date _____

Name _____
Assignment _____

Name _____
Assignment _____

Name _____
Assignment _____

Standards-Based LANGUAGE ARTS Graphic Organizers, Rubrics, and Writing Prompts for Middle Grade Students

Copyright ©2001 by Incentive Publications, Inc. Nashville, TN.

Illustrated Booklet Assessment

Rating Scale

1 = Excellent	3 = Fair
2 = Good	4 = Poor

1. Quality of Report Format   Rating: _____

My booklet contains at least 16 important facts related to my topic with appropriate illustrations for each fact or idea. I have used one key idea or fact per page accompanied by a title page and a short test.

2. Quality of Information   Rating: _____

My material is well-researched and conveys important information on my topic.

3. Interest   Rating: _____

My writing is interesting to read and the illustrations hold the reader's attention.

4. Grammar   Rating: _____

There are no errors in grammar, punctuation, and spelling in my report.

5. Graphics/Creativity   Rating: _____

The illustrations are appropriate for illustrating the information I have selected about my topic.

6. Reflection   Rating: _____

Overall I think my rating for this piece of work should be _____ .

Comments by Student: _____

_____

_____

        Signed _____ Date _____

Comments by Teacher: _____

_____

_____

        Signed _____ Date _____

Independent Project Assessment

Absolutely = ☆ ☆ ☆   Somewhat = ☆ ☆   Not so good = ☆

1. My topic was well-selected and appropriate for an independent study.	Rating: _____
2. My thoughts, ideas, and information are presented in a logical, sequential manner.	Rating: _____
3. The vocabulary is interesting and is composed of words I understand and know how to use.	Rating: _____
4. I have eliminated unnecessary, confusing, irrelevant, redundant, or trite sentences and phrases from my work.	Rating: _____
5. I have used some unusual or extraordinary descriptive words or phrases to add interest to my work.	Rating: _____
6. I have used examples, illustrations, graphic organizers, and/or analogies to explain or clarify main ideas or important concepts.	Rating: _____
7. I have included necessary information and related details and eliminated unnecessary or irrelevant facts in order to make the report lively and relevant.	Rating: _____
8. I have included a good balance of different kinds of sentences to maintain the reader's interest throughout my work.	Rating: _____
9. I have checked my spelling, grammar, and punctuation carefully.	Rating: _____
10. The culmination or wrap-up of my project is interesting enough to leave my reader with a better understanding of my subject, some new ideas, and/or thoughts to ponder.	Rating: _____
11. My writing is neat, clear, and easy to read.	Rating: _____
12. This project is representative of my absolute best work.	Rating: _____

Project Topic: _____

Project Title: _____

Total Score (circle):   ☆ ☆ ☆   ☆ ☆   ☆

Comments by Student: _____

_____

Signed _____ Date _____

Comments by Teacher: _____

_____

Signed _____ Date _____

Standards-Based LANGUAGE ARTS Graphic Organizers, Rubrics, and Writing Prompts for Middle Grade Students

Independent Reading Assessment

My independent reading includes a good balance of fiction and non-fiction.

           Poor   Good   Excellent

My independent reading includes reading for pleasure, for information, and for entertainment.

           Poor   Good   Excellent

When I encounter a new word whose meaning I do not know, I use a dictionary or reference source to look it up.

           Poor   Good   Excellent

I have a friend or friends with whom I regularly discuss books I read and exchange recommendations for good books.

           Poor   Good   Excellent

I spend at least 45–90 minutes a day reading materials other than those included in my regular school assignments.

           Poor   Good   Excellent

If given a choice between reading a good book, watching a television program or playing a computer game, I choose to

_____ .

Standards-Based LANGUAGE ARTS Graphic Organizers, Rubrics, and Writing Prompts for Middle Grade Students

I do __ or do not __ have a library lending card in my own name.

One improvement I need to make in my independent reading plan is

_____

_____

_____

_____

The best thing about my independent reading habits is

_____

_____

_____

_____

I would say that my independent reading habits are

Poor	Good	Excellent

Summary : _____

_____

_____

_____

_____

_____

_____

Name: _____ Date _____

Standards-Based LANGUAGE ARTS Graphic Organizers, Rubrics, and Writing Prompts for Middle Grade Students

Journal Assessment

Rating Scale:

4	3	2	1
Slow Down	Keep Going	Right On	WOW

1. Quality of Report Format   Rating: _____

My journal report records are dated entries about my topic including important events, activities, feelings, reactions to information, observations, experiences, summaries, and conclusions.

2. Quality of Information   Rating: _____

My journal is well researched and conveys important and accurate information on my topic.

3. Details and Descriptions   Rating: _____

I have used colorful vocabulary and original thought to present details and descriptions in a lively manner.

4. Grammar   Rating: _____

There are no errors in the grammar and spelling of my report.

5. Interest   Rating: _____

My report is interesting to read and holds the reader's attention.

6. Graphics/Creativity   Rating: _____

The information in my report is creatively organized and presented.

Comments by Student: _____

_____

_____

_____

Signed _____ Date _____

Comments by Teacher: _____

_____

_____

_____

Signed _____ Date _____

Standards-Based LANGUAGE ARTS Graphic Organizers, Rubrics, and Writing Prompts for Middle Grade Students

Learning Poster
Assessment Rubric Based on
Gardner's Eight Multiple Intelligences

Rating Scale: Yes   Kind Of   No

1. Quality of Report Format: Rating: _____

My Learning Poster is a large poster containing eight sections,
one for each Multiple Intelligence approach to my topic/subject.

2. Use of Prior Knowledge: Rating: _____

I was able to use previously acquired knowledge and understanding of the eight multiple
intelligences as identified by Howard Gardner to plan and complete my poster.

3. Quality of Information: Rating: _____

The organization of information in my Learning Poster
makes logical sense and it covers my topic well.

4. Evidence of Creativity: Rating: _____

My Learning Poster conveys sequentially organized information
visually in an original and effective way.

5. Quality of Layout and Graphics: Rating: _____

My Learning Poster uses layout and graphics to make my topic
easier to understand and interesting to read.

6. Grammar: Rating: _____

My Learning Poster contains no grammar, spelling, or punctuation errors.

Student Reflection and Evaluation: _____

_____

Signed _____ Date _____

Comments by Teacher: _____

_____

Signed _____ Date _____

Letter Report Assessment

Rating Scale: 1st Class Stamp = Excellent   3rd Class Stamp = Fair

2nd Class Stamp = Good   Bulk Mail = No evidence

Elements to Be Evaluated	1	2	3	B
1. Quality of Report Format My report includes a series of letters to the same person conveying information on my topic.				
2. Quality of Form I followed the proper form for letter writing in all my letters.				
3. Quality of Information The topic information is factual and is conveyed in as many letters as necessary.				
4. Interest The main points of my topic are explained personally yet informatively, and my letters follow a logical sequence.				
5. Grammar There are no spelling or grammar errors in my report.				
6. Graphics/Creativity The graphics and designs on my stationery help communicate the topic information.				
7. Overall Rating				

Comments by Student: _____

_____

_____

Signed _____ Date _____

Comments by Teacher: _____

_____

_____

Signed _____ Date _____

*Standards-Based LANGUAGE ARTS Graphic Organizers,
Rubrics, and Writing Prompts for Middle Grade Students*

Magazine or Newspaper Report Assessment

	Rating Scale:	Best	OK	Needs Work
		STAR WRITER	STAFF WRITER	INTERN WRITER
1. Quality of Information The information in my magazine or newspaper report demonstrates thorough research into my subject using a variety of resources.				
2. Magazine Article or Newspaper Format My report includes a banner headline and several sections.				
3. Grammar There are no spelling or grammar errors in my magazine or newspaper report and it is neatly written.				
4. Interest The different sections of my magazine or newspaper report present the main points of my subject and explain them well.				
5. Graphics/Creativity The newspaper layout and illustrations are attractive and convey information on my topic.				
6. Coverage My topic is presented in a complete and concise manner to give the reader a good understanding of the subject.				

Comments by Student: _____

_____

_____

Signed _____ Date _____

Comments by Teacher: _____

_____

_____

Signed _____ Date _____

Matrix Assessment

Rating Scale:

1	2	3
Best	Next Best	Keep Working

---

1. Quality of Report Format   Rating: _____

The Matrix Report includes appropriate categories and information in rows and columns.

2. Quality of Information   Rating: _____

The information in my report demonstrates significant research into the topic.

3. Grammar   Rating: _____

There are no spelling or grammar errors in my report.

4. Interest   Rating: _____

The different elements and comparative features in my matrix highlight the main points of my topic and explain the topic well.

5. Graphics/Creativity   Rating: _____

The layout and selection of information is creative and original.

Comments by Student: _____

_____

_____

_____

_____

Signed _____ Date _____

Comments by Teacher: _____

_____

_____

_____

_____

Signed _____ Date _____

Standards-Based LANGUAGE ARTS Graphic Organizers,
Rubrics, and Writing Prompts for Middle Grade Students

Project or Portfolio Review and Reflection Guide

Reflection is an important part of the learning process. Only the skills and concepts that are internalized and processed are available for use to remember and use in the future. Review and reflect on your group project or portfolio. Use the following questions to help you.

1. **Was my project or portfolio based on meaningful goals, and well planned to carry out the goals?**

   _____

   _____

2. **Did I plan and carry out my work according to a realistic timeline?**

   _____

   _____

3. **What do I know now that I did not know before?**

   _____

   _____

4. **What can I do now that I could not do before?**

   _____

   _____

5. **What did I learn that will help me learn more or will inspire me to do further reading or study?**

   _____

   _____

Standards-Based LANGUAGE ARTS Graphic Organizers, Rubrics, and Writing Prompts for Middle Grade Students

6. What are strengths of my work?

_____

_____

7. What could I have done better?

_____

_____

8. What was the most interesting part of the work?

_____

_____

9. Does the work show a creative approach?

_____

_____

10. Using A for excellent. B for good, C for acceptable and D for barely or not acceptable, what letter grade would I give myself, and why?

_____

_____

11. What would I do differently if I were doing this project again?

_____

_____

_Standards-Based LANGUAGE ARTS Graphic Organizers,
Rubrics, and Writing Prompts for Middle Grade Students_

Public Speech Performance Assessment

Rating Scale	1st Place	2nd Place	3rd Place	4th Place
Circle your rating.	Red Hot Speech	Hot	Warm	Cold

Delivering a speech is not as easy as it sounds. Here is how I rate my performance:

1.
My purpose for the speech was clear and I was committed to the topic.

Rating: _____

2.
I took the time to organize my thought, research my topic, and have all my materials ready well in advance of my speech.

Rating: _____

3.
I rehearsed my speech until I thought I was ready to give a perfect performance.

Rating: _____

4.
I used appropriate gestures, body language, and good posture and conveyed confidence.

Rating: _____

5.
I established eye contact with my audience.

Rating: _____

6.
I projected my voice and spoke pleasantly, loudly, and clearly.

Rating: _____

7.
I anticipated questions that might be asked and prepared myself with possible answers.

Rating: _____

8.
I began and ended my speech with statements to capture the audience's attention and to leave them with thoughts to hold and to ponder.

Rating: _____

9.
On the whole, I think my speech was:

_____

10. If I were doing it again I would:

_____

Signed _____ Date _____

Teacher feedback: On the whole I think your speech was: _____

If you were giving it again you could: _____

Signed _____ Date _____

Standards-Based LANGUAGE ARTS Graphic Organizers, Rubrics, and Writing Prompts for Middle Grade Students

Research Project Assessment

	Best	Better	Good	Fair	Poor
1. Quality of Project Format My research project is composed of a series of notebook or file card entries presenting my assigned topic, with each properly dated and sourced.	1	2	3	4	5
2. Quality of Information My notes show significant research, using a variety of resources.	1	2	3	4	5
3. Quality of Documentation My sources are fully and properly documented, including complete bibliographical information.	1	2	3	4	5
4. Grammar I checked my work carefully and it is free of spelling and grammar errors.	1	2	3	4	5
5. Interest The items in my research project are diverse and appropriate for presenting key information and/or special highlights about the topic.	1	2	3	4	5
6. Graphics/Creativity The design, layout, and graphics/illustrations are creative and effective.	1	2	3	4	5

Comments by Student: _____

_____

_____

_____

Signed _____ Date _____

Comments by Teacher: _____

_____

_____

_____

Signed _____ Date _____

Tape-Recorded Project Assessment

1. Quality of Report Format

Off Target   Pretty Close   Near Miss   Bull's Eye

My report is an audio recording of notes from my research on my topic, explaining key definitions, events, and concepts.

2. Quality of Information

Off Target   Pretty Close   Near Miss   Bull's Eye

The data in my report is well-researched and presented logically.

3. Vocabulary

Off Target   Pretty Close   Near Miss   Bull's Eye

My report contains colorful and descriptive vocabulary and language.

4. Grammar

Off Target   Pretty Close   Near Miss   Bull's Eye

My report and my note cards contain no spelling or grammar errors.

5. Interest

Off Target   Pretty Close   Near Miss   Bull's Eye

My report makes my topic easier to understand and interesting to learn about.

6. Graphics/Creativity

Off Target   Pretty Close   Near Miss   Bull's Eye

My report is given with a clear and engaging voice, as well as connections and pauses between notecards.

7. Audience Appeal

Off Target   Pretty Close   Near Miss   Bull's Eye

My report will capture and hold the interest of the intended audience.

Comments by Student: _____

_____

_____

Signed _____ Date _____

Comments by Teacher: _____

_____

_____

Signed _____ Date _____

Rubric
_____

Term Paper Assessment

Title: _____

| Rating Scale: | 3 superior | 2 good | 1 acceptable | 0 not acceptable |

	STUDENT RATING	TEACHER RATING
1. Choice of Topic		
2. Quality of Resources		
3. Objectives		
4. Quality of Research		
5. Organization		
6. Knowledge of Subject		
7. Attention to Details		
8. Accuracy of Information		
9. Grammar, Punctuation, Spelling		
10. Imagination or Creativity		
11. Neatness and Graphics		
12. Evidence of Best Effort		

*Standards-Based LANGUAGE ARTS Graphic Organizers,
Rubrics, and Writing Prompts for Middle Grade Students*

Term Paper Assessment (cont.)

The best thing about this paper was: _____

_____

_____

_____

_____

_____

_____

_____

One thing that could have made it better was: _____

_____

_____

_____

_____

_____

_____

_____

Student Signature: _____

Teacher Signature: _____

Date of Evaluation: _____

Visual Aid Assessment

Rating Scale	Best of Show I	Good Show II	Fair Show III	Poor Show IV

1. Quality of Presentation Format   Rating: _____
Oral presentation uses visual aids related to the presentation and of high interest.

2. Quality of Information   Rating: _____
Oral presentation is well researched and visual aids enhance and support the information presented.

3. Grammar   Rating: _____
Grammar and pronunciation of oral presentation and grammar and spelling of identification and/or descriptive tags or labels for visual aids is correct.

4. Interest   Rating: _____
Visual aids and oral presentation are well integrated, smoothly presented, interesting, clear, and informative.

5. Graphics/Creativity   Rating: _____
Visual aids are creatively chosen, ordered, and presented to convey topic information and add interest to the presentation.

6. Reflection   Rating: _____
Upon reflection, the visual aids used for this presentation were the best aids I could have used to hold my audience's attention and to convey the facts and information in a meaningful way.

Comments by Student: _____

_____

Signed _____ Date _____

Comments by Teacher: _____

_____

Signed _____ Date _____

Vocabulary Development Assessment

1. **I can pronounce and tell the meaning of at least twenty new vocabulary words.**   Rating: _____

2. **I can recognize these words when I see them in print, and can easily identify them in puzzles, games, signs, and on the T.V. screen.**   Rating: _____

3. **I can use these words in context in my own writing.**   Rating: _____

4. **I can use these words confidently in conversation.**   Rating: _____

5. **I can spell these words.**   Rating: _____

6. **I can safely say that I have added these words to my listening, speaking, reading, and writing vocabulary.**   Rating: _____

Comments by Student: _____

_____

_____

_____

Signed _____ Date _____

Comments by Teacher: _____

_____

_____

_____

Signed _____ Date _____

Student Teacher
Evaluation Conference

Rating Scale:

1. Quality of Report Format The format selected for this work is appropriate for the content.	**Rating:** _____
2. Quality of Information My information is well researched.	**Rating:** _____
3. Grammar My work contains no grammar or spelling errors	**Rating:** _____
4. Interest My work's layout and graphics make my topic easier to understand and interesting to read about.	**Rating:** _____
5. Graphics/Creativity My work conveys information in an original and effective way.	**Rating:** _____

Comments by Student: _____

_____

_____

_____

Signed _____ Date _____

Comments by Teacher: _____

_____

_____

_____

Signed _____ Date _____

Standards-Based LANGUAGE ARTS Graphic Organizers,
Rubrics, and Writing Prompts for Middle Grade Students

Student Assessment of Rubrics
As A Means of Measuring Student
Progress and/or as an Option for
More Traditional Assessment Tools

Directions: Circle one ([are] or [are not]) in statements 1–7 below and 9 on page 123. Complete the other statements as appropriate.

1. I think rubrics [are] or [are not] a good tool for assessment because:

   _____

   _____

2. I think letter grades such as A B C D F [are] or [are not] a fair way to assess the quality of a language arts performance based task because:

   _____

   _____

3. In my opinion, multiple choice tests [are] or [are not] a good assessment tool for language arts programs because:

   _____

   _____

4. In my opinion, teacher-made tests [are] or [are not] a good assessment tool for language arts programs because:

   _____

   _____

5. In my opinion, standardized tests [are] or [are not] a good assessment tool for language arts programs because:

   _____

   _____

6. In my opinion, essay-type tests [are] or [are not] a good assessment tool for language arts programs because:

   _____

   _____

7. In my opinion, true/false tests [are] or [are not] a good assessment tool for language arts programs because:

   _____

   _____

8. If given a choice between teacher-made, true/false tests, essay type questions, multiple choice tests, or rubrics as an assessment to determine my language arts grade, I would choose

   _____ because:

   _____

   _____

9. I think the teacher comments [are] or [are not] an important part of rubric assessment form because:

_____

_____

10. I think my parents [understand] or [do not understand] *(circle one)* the use of rubrics as an assessment tool and view them as [important] or [not important] *(circle one)* in gaining a better understanding of my progress in language arts.

11. I think rubrics help me to communicate [more effectively] or [less effectively] *(circle one)* with my teacher and, therefore, to measure my own progress in language arts [more] or [less] *(circle one)* than do traditional pencil and paper quizzes or end-of-chapter test questions.

12. The strengths and weaknesses of rubrics as a quantitative measure of my progress in language arts as I see them are:

Strengths: _____

_____

_____

Weaknesses: _____

_____

On the whole, I would rate their value as an assessment tool as currently used in our language arts program as: *(circle one)*

Extremely Valuable: Meaning and intent is clear, provides pertinent information for planning further study, and points out strengths and weaknesses of my work

Somewhat Valuable: Provides some insights to my progress and grasp of the knowledge and concepts studied, helps me to evaluate my performance, and plan for future study

Not Very Valuable: Meaning and intent are "fuzzy"; feedback is not especially relative and gives me little concrete information about my overall progress or help in planning for improvement of future work

In a summary statement of three sentences or less, I would say rubrics as a language arts assessment tool are:

_____

_____

_____

_____

_____

*Standards-Based LANGUAGE ARTS Graphic Organizers,
Rubrics, and Writing Prompts for Middle Grade Students*

Questions for Teachers and Students to Consider About Using Rubrics in the Classroom

1. What is a rubric and what kinds of rubrics are there?

   _____

2. What are some characteristics of effective rubrics?

   _____

3. What are the critical components in the design of rubrics?

   _____

4. What is a holistic rubric?

   _____

5. What is an analytical rubric?

   _____

6. Are rubrics developed by students, by teachers, or both?

   _____

7. How does one decide on the criteria of a given rubric?

   _____

8. How does one determine the best type of rating scale for a given rubric?

   _____

9. Are rubrics appropriate for all types of instruction and all types of content areas?

   _____

10. How does one teach students to use and value rubrics as an assessment tool?

    _____

11. Why are rubrics an effective way to measure student performance?

    _____

12. Are rubrics appropriate for measuring the quality of a student-generated product?

    _____

13. How does one translate the results of a rubric into a numerical grade?

    _____

14. How does one use rubrics to guide evaluation and establish a shared standard of quality work?

    _____

15. Are the development and use of rubrics more time consuming for students and teachers as an assessment tool and, if so, is that time commitment worth the effort?

    _____

Standards-Based LANGUAGE ARTS Graphic Organizers, Rubrics, and Writing Prompts for Middle Grade Students

Appendix

English/Language Arts Standards for Grades K-8

Planning Matrix

Create Your Own Rubric

Writing Prompts for Grammar Reinforcement

Gardner's Multiple Intelligences

Calendar for Using Graphic Organizers

Calendar for Writing Prompts

Performance Project or Task
Independent Study Contract

Bloom's Taxonomy of Cognitive Thinking Skills

Bibliography

Index

International Reading Association/
National Council of Teachers of English

English/Language Arts Standards
Grades K-8

Standard 1:

Students read a wide range of print and nonprint text to build an understanding of texts, of themselves, and of the cultures of the United States and the world, to acquire new information, to respond to the needs and demands of society and the workplace, and for personal fulfillment. Among these texts are fiction and nonfiction, classic and contemporary works.

Standard 2:

Students read a wide range of literature from many periods in many genres to build an understanding of the many dimensions (e.g. philosophical, ethical, aesthetic) of human experience.

Standard 3:

Students apply a wide range of strategies to comprehend, interpret, evaluate, and appreciate texts. They draw on their prior experience, their interactions with other readers and writers, their knowledge of word meaning and of other texts, their identification strategies, and their understanding of textual features (e.g., sound-letter correspondence, sentence structure, context, graphics).

Standard 4:

Students adjust their use of spoken, written, and visual language (e.g., conventions, style, vocabulary) to communicate effectively with a variety of audiences for a variety of purposes.

Standard 5:

Students employ a wide range of strategies as they write and use different writing process elements appropriately to communicate with different audiences for a variety of purposes.

Standards-Based LANGUAGE ARTS Graphic Organizers, Rubrics, and Writing Prompts for Middle Grade Students

Copyright ©2001 by Incentive Publications, Inc.
Nashville, TN.

Standard 6:

Students apply knowledge of language structure, language conventions (e.g., spelling and punctuation), media techniques, figurative language, and genre to create, critique, and discuss print and non-print texts.

Standard 7:

Students conduct research on issues and interests by generating ideas and questions, and by posing problems. They gather, evaluate, and synthesize data from a variety of sources (e.g., print and non-print texts, artifacts, people) to communicate their discoveries in ways that suit their purpose and audience.

Standard 8:

Students use a variety of technological and informational resources (e.g., libraries, databases, computer networks, video) to gather and synthesize information and to create and to communicate knowledge.

Standard 9:

Students develop an understanding of and respect for diversity in language use, patterns, and dialects across cultures, ethnic groups, geographic regions, and social roles.

Standard 10:

Students whose first language is not English make use of their first language to develop competency in the English language arts and to develop understanding of content across the curriculum.

Standard 11:

Students participate as knowledgeable, reflective, creative, and critical members of a variety of literacy communities.

Standard 12:

Students use spoken, written, and visual language to accomplish their own purposes (e.g., for learning, enjoyment, persuasion, and the exchange of information).

Standards for the English Language Arts, by the International Reading Association and the National Council of Teachers of English, Copyright 1996 by the International Reading Association and the National Council of Teachers of English. Reprinted with permission.

*Standards-Based LANGUAGE ARTS Graphic Organizers,
Rubrics, and Writing Prompts for Middle Grade Students*

Planning Matrix

Correlatives: National Language Arts Standards as identified by the National Council of Teachers of English and the International Reading Association with activities and projects in Standards-Based Graphic Organizers, Rubrics, and Writing Prompts, Incentive Publications, 2001.

Standards	Graphic Organizers	Writing Prompts	Rubrics	Reinforcement & Reflection
STANDARD 1: Students read a wide range of print and nonprint text to build an understanding of texts, of themselves, and of the cultures of the United States and the world, to acquire new information, to respond to the needs and demands of society and the workplace, and for personal fulfillment. Among these texts are fiction and nonfiction, classic and contemporary works.	12, 13, 14, 15, 16, 17, 18, 19, 20, 29, 32, 33, 35, 36, 37, 38, 40, 41, 43, 44, 45	60, 61, 65, 68, 69, 78, 79, 81, 83	96, 101, 102, 104, 107, 117, 118	12, 17, 20, 29, 38, 44, 45, 60, 100
STANDARD 2: Students read a wide range of literature from many periods in many genres to build an understanding of the many dimensions (e.g. philosophical, ethical, aesthetic) of human experience.	12, 15, 19, 20, 21, 22, 25, 26, 29, 35, 36, 42, 44, 46, 49, 54, 57	60, 61, 66, 67, 73, 75, 76, 80, 84	92, 101, 102, 104, 105, 106	12, 19, 26, 29, 42, 57, 58, 61
STANDARD 3: Students apply a wide range of strategies to comprehend, interpret, evaluate, and appreciate texts. They draw on their prior experience, their interactions with other readers and writers, their knowledge of word meaning and of other texts, their identification strategies, and their understanding of textual features (e.g., sound-letter correspondence, sentence structure, context, graphics).	13, 15, 17, 18, 19, 21, 22, 26, 35, 36, 38, 40, 43, 46, 49, 56	61, 63, 64, 65, 71, 72, 75, 78, 82, 108	93, 95, 96, 97, 98, 104, 107, 109, 112, 113, 119	16, 17, 21, 37, 38, 46, 60, 61, 86, 87, 100, 102, 110, 114
STANDARD 4: Students adjust their use of spoken, written, and visual language (e.g., conventions, style, vocabulary) to communicate effectively with a variety of audiences for a variety of purposes.	13, 14, 15, 16, 17, 18, 19, 20, 24, 31, 33, 35, 36, 37, 38, 40, 42, 45, 53	60, 63, 64, 65, 66, 67, 74, 75	93, 95, 97, 99, 101, 103, 114	10, 11, 17, 20, 28, 39, 45, 58, 100, 102, 112, 113, 120

Planning Matrix

Correlatives: National Language Arts Standards as identified by the National Council of Teachers of English and the International Reading Association with activities and projects in Standards-Based Graphic Organizers, Rubrics, and Writing Prompts, Incentive Publications, 2001.

Standards	Graphic Organizers	Writing Prompts	Rubrics	Reinforcement & Reflection
STANDARD 5: Students employ a wide range of strategies as they write and use different writing process elements appropriately to communicate with different audiences for a variety of purposes.	12, 13, 17, 18, 20, 21, 22, 25, 29, 31, 38, 40, 45, 46, 47, 49, 55	61, 63, 64, 66, 69, 71, 73, 74, 79, 81	93, 95, 98, 100, 103, 109, 110, 112, 113	13, 17, 20, 22, 31, 39, 45, 49, 122, 123
STANDARD 6: Students apply knowledge of language structure, language conventions (e.g., spelling and punctuation), media techniques, figurative language, and genre to create, critique, and discuss print and non-print texts.	11, 12, 13, 14, 15, 16, 17, 19, 20, 22, 23, 25, 28, 29, 30, 31, 33, 34, 35, 36, 37, 39, 43, 45, 48, 51, 54	61, 62, 63, 65, 67, 68, 69, 70, 72, 73, 74, 76, 77, 78, 79, 80, 81, 85, 107	92, 94, 95, 98, 100, 103, 109, 110, 114, 117, 118, 119	10, 11, 14, 16, 17, 19, 20, 22, 28, 33, 34, 37, 39, 43, 45, 48, 60, 86, 87, 112, 113, 120
STANDARD 7: Students conduct research on issues and interests by generating ideas and questions, and by posing problems. They gather, evaluate, and synthesize data from a variety of sources (e.g., print and non-print texts, artifacts, people) to communicate their discoveries in ways that suit their purpose and audience.	11, 12, 14, 15, 17, 18, 20, 21, 22, 23, 25, 28, 29, 30, 34, 35, 36, 40, 41, 46, 47, 49, 50, 55	62, 65, 66, 67, 68, 70, 78, 82, 85	93, 96, 98, 101, 103, 104, 110, 111, 115, 116, 117, 118	10, 12, 15, 18, 20, 21, 23, 29, 35, 41, 44, 47, 50, 58, 119
STANDARD 8: Students use a variety of technological and informational resources (e.g., libraries, databases, computer networks, video) to gather and synthesize information and to create and to communicate knowledge.	11, 12, 13, 14, 15, 18, 25, 28, 29, 30, 31, 34, 35, 36, 40, 55	66, 67, 68, 78, 80, 82, 85	92, 94, 96, 110, 111, 115, 116, 117, 118	13, 15, 32, 35, 58

Standards-Based LANGUAGE ARTS Graphic Organizers, Rubrics, and Writing Prompts for Middle Grade Students

Planning Matrix

Correlatives: National Language Arts Standards as identified by the National Council of Teachers of English and the International Reading Association with activities and projects in Standards-Based Graphic Organizers, Rubrics, and Writing Prompts, Incentive Publications, 2001.

Standards	Graphic Organizers	Writing Prompts	Rubrics	Reinforcement & Reflection
STANDARD 9: Students develop an understanding of and respect for diversity in language use, patterns, and dialects across cultures, ethnic groups, geographic regions, and social roles.	14, 16, 17, 18, 19, 20, 24, 26, 33, 37, 38, 41, 43, 44, 52, 56, 57	61, 63, 69, 70, 78, 83	92, 99, 102, 120	14, 17, 20, 26, 33, 34, 38, 44, 45, 56, 61
STANDARD 10: Students whose first language is not English make use of their first language to develop competency in the English language arts and to develop understanding of content across the curriculum.	12, 13, 15, 16, 17, 19, 20, 21, 24, 26, 29, 32, 35, 36, 37, 38, 43, 45, 46, 53, 56, 57	60, 61, 62, 63, 66, 83	99, 100, 104, 117, 118, 120	12, 15, 19, 20, 26, 29, 32, 35, 43, 45, 57, 61, 62
STANDARD 11: Students participate as knowledgeable, reflective, creative, and critical members of a variety of literacy communities.	12, 13, 16, 17, 18, 19, 20, 22, 23, 24, 25, 26, 29, 31, 37, 39, 40, 41, 43, 44, 45, 49, 50, 53, 55, 57	63, 64, 66, 69, 70, 71, 72, 76, 83, 84	92, 99, 100, 114	11, 13, 17, 18, 19, 20, 22, 28, 31, 38, 41, 43, 45, 49, 60, 86, 87, 100, 105, 109
STANDARD 12: Students use spoken, written, and visual language to accomplish their own purposes (e.g., for learning, enjoyment, persuasion, and the exchange of information).	12, 14, 16, 17, 18, 19, 20, 21, 22, 23, 24, 25, 26, 29, 34, 37, 39, 40, 41, 43, 44, 45, 46, 48, 49, 51, 53, 55, 56	60, 61, 62, 63, 64, 65, 69, 70, 71, 72, 73, 75, 76, 78, 79, 84	92, 95, 99, 100, 101, 104, 105, 106, 108, 116, 117, 118, 119, 120, 122, 123	10, 12, 17, 18, 20, 21, 23, 24, 25, 29, 39, 40, 45, 49, 51, 55, 58, 60, 61, 86, 87, 121

Standards-Based LANGUAGE ARTS Graphic Organizers, Rubrics, and Writing Prompts for Middle Grade Students

Criteria for Creating Your Own Rubric

Excellent

My portfolio, project, or task
1. is complete.
2. is well-organized.
3. is visually exciting.
4. shows much evidence of multiple resources.
5. shows much evidence of problem solving, decision making, and higher-order thinking skills.
6. reflects enthusiasm for the subject.
7. contains additional work beyond the requirements.
8. communicates effectively what I have learned in keeping with my learning objectives.
9. includes highly efficient assessment tools and makes ample provisions for meta cognitive reflection.
10. has identified many future learning goals in keeping with my own needs and interests.

Good

My portfolio, project, or task
1. is complete.
2. is well-organized.
3. is interesting.
4. shows some evidence of multiple resources.
5. shows some evidence of problem solving, decision making, and higher-order thinking skills.
6. reflects some interest for the topic.
7. contains a small amount of work beyond the requirements.
8. communicates some things I have learned in keeping with my learning objectives.
9. includes effective assessment tools and reflective comments.
10. has identified some future learning goals in keeping with my own needs and interests.

Needs Improvement

My portfolio, project, or task
1. is incomplete.
2. is poorly organized.
3. is not very interesting to others.
4. shows little or almost no evidence of multiple resources.
5. shows little or almost no evidence of problem solving, decision making, and higher-order thinking skills.
6. reflects little interest in the subject.
7. contains no additional work beyond the minimum requirements.
8. communicates few things that I have truly learned in keeping with my objectives.
9. includes few examples of self assessment tools and reflective comments.
10. has identified no future learning goals in keeping with my own needs and interests.

Standards-Based LANGUAGE ARTS Graphic Organizers,
Rubrics, and Writing Prompts for Middle Grade Students

Outline for Creating Your Own Rubric

Directions: Use this outline and the criteria for creating your own rubric, project, or task. A holistic rubric assigns levels of performance with descriptors for each level. An analytic rubric assigns levels of performance with numerical points allocated for every descriptor at each level.

Excellent Levels

Descriptors: Points Awarded:

_____   _____

_____   _____

_____   _____

Good Levels

Descriptors: Points Awarded:

_____   _____

_____   _____

_____   _____

Needs Improvement

Descriptors: Points Awarded:

_____   _____

_____   _____

_____   _____

Note: You can add additional levels and descriptors as needed. You can also create your own labels for the levels and use such categories as: Exemplary Achievement, Commendable Achievement, Limited Evidence of Achievement, and Minimal Achievement.

Comments by Student: _____

_____

Signed _____ Date _____

Comments by Teacher: _____

_____

Signed _____ Date _____

Standards-Based LANGUAGE ARTS Graphic Organizers, Rubrics, and Writing Prompts for Middle Grade Students

Writing Prompts to Stir the Imagination and Make Journal Entries for a Study of Grammar More Interesting

1. Create an editorial cartoon illustrating some aspect of how grammar is taught in your classroom.

2. Make a list of ten interesting proper nouns, ten common nouns, and ten verbs. Write a paragraph on a subject of interest to you using as many of them as you can.

3. Explain the difference between a subject and a predicate.

4. Define adjectives and adverbs and tell why they are important to creative writing.

5. Tell why you think grammar is important to a student of your age, an engineer, a musician, a T.V. reporter, and a teacher. Which one of these people do you feel would be most handicapped by a poor understanding of grammar rules and use?

6. Would you say you are more like a question mark, a comma, a period, a semi-colon, or an exclamation mark? Explain your answer.

7. Name the parts of speech and give three good reasons why it is important to learn them.

8. Just for fun, tell what you think the consequences would be of a ban on teaching grammar in all middle schools across the country.

9. If you were asked to write a letter giving advice to a student from another country, who is just beginning to study the English language, what are the most important things you would suggest?

10. Write a critique of your English textbook with special emphasis on grammar. Are the lessons interesting as well as informative?

11. Are you able to use what you are learning about grammar for writing across the curriculum to improve your overall rate of school success?

12. Write a letter to your English teacher telling the one thing you like best about the assignments required as part of the class and suggesting one change only that you would like to see made in future assignments.

13. Design a billboard based on one specific grammar rule. Use graphics and catchy phrases to make it interesting to people of all ages.

Gardner's Multiple Intelligences

Did you know there are eight different types of intelligence and that each of us possesses all eight, although one or more of them may be stronger than others? Dr. Howard Gardner, a researcher and professor at the Harvard Graduate School of Education, has developed the Theory of Multiple Intelligences to help us better understand ourselves and the way we acquire information in school. Try to rank order the eight intelligences below as they best describe the way you learn, with "1" being your strongest intelligence area and "8" being your weakest intelligence area. Try to think of examples and instances in the classroom when you were successful on a test, assignment, activity, or task because it was compatible with the way you like to learn.

_____ 1. **Linguistic Intelligence:** Do you find it easy to memorize information, write poems or stories, give oral talks, read books, play word games like Scrabble and Password, use big words in your conversations or assignments, and remember what you hear?

_____ 2. **Logical-Mathematical Intelligence:** Do you find it easy to compute numbers in your head and on paper, to solve brain teasers, to do logic puzzles, to conduct science experiments, to figure out number and sequence patterns, and to watch videos or television shows on science and nature themes?

_____ 3. **Spatial Intelligence:** Do you find it easy to draw, paint, or doodle, work through puzzles and mazes, build with blocks or various types of buildings sets, follow maps and flow charts, use a camera to record what you see around you, and prefer reading material that has lots of illustrations?

_____ 4. **Bodily-Kinesthetic Intelligence:** Do you find it easy to engage in lots of sports and physical activities, move around rather than sit still, spend free time outdoors, work with your hands on such things as model-building or sewing, participate in dance, ballet, gymnastics, plays, puppet shows or other performances, and mess around with finger painting, clay, and paper-mache?

_____ 5. **Musical Intelligence:** Do you find it easy to play a musical instrument or sing in the choir, listen to favorite records or tapes, make up your own songs or raps, recognize off-key recordings or noises, remember television jingles and lyrics of many different songs, and work while listening to or humming simple melodies and tunes?

_____ 6. **Interpersonal Intelligence:** Do you find it easy to make friends, meet strangers, resolve conflicts among peers, lead groups or clubs, engage in gossip, participate in team sports, plan social activities, and teach or counsel others?

_____ 7. **Intrapersonal Intelligence:** Do you find it easy to function independently, do your own work and thinking, spend time alone, engage in solo hobbies and activities, attend personal growth seminars, set goals, analyze your own strengths and weaknesses, and keep private diaries or journals?

_____ 8. **Naturalist Intelligence:** Do you find yourself extremely comfortable and happy outdoors, have a desire to explore and observe the environment, use outdoor equipment such as binoculars easily, and want to understand how natural systems evolve and how things work?

Standards-Based LANGUAGE ARTS Graphic Organizers, Rubrics, and Writing Prompts for Middle Grade Students

Sample Multiple Intelligences Activity
Creative Writing, Thinking and Speaking

Verbal/Linguistic
Write your own definition of creativity. Explain how a person can recognize a creative idea in his or her writing, thinking, or speaking.

Logical/Mathematical
Think about the most creative people you know in your class or in your school. What special traits do these people demonstrate in writing, thinking, and/or speaking?

Visual/Spatial
Draw a picture or diagram that shows your ideas about what creativity is and is not.

Body/Kinesthetic
Write an original poem, skit, short story, tall tale, myth, fairy tale, or legend. Act out your words through creative dramatics.

Musical/Rhythmic
Enhance your original writing in the Body/Kinesthetic activity with appropriate sounds or rhythm.

Interpersonal
Plan and conduct a panel discussion on the topic of creativity in the classroom. Identify the types of classroom climate, assignments, tasks, tools, and resources that promote or inhibit creative acts by students. Discuss whether creativity is inherited and innate or whether it can be taught and nurtured.

Intrapersonal
Rate your personal ability to write, think, and speak creatively when given classroom assignments, using a 1 to 10 scale. Consider 1 as "very low in creativity," 5 as "somewhat creative," and 10 as "highly creative." Give reasons for your rating decisions.

Naturalist
Create a nature walk, trail, or other outdoor classroom activity geared towards observing nature through using each of the five senses. Share with your findings with peers, by leading them on a guided tour.

A Calendar of Integrated Learning Activities to Reinforce the Use of Graphic Organizers

	Monday	Tuesday	Wednesday	Thursday	Friday
Knowledge Comprehension	Use magazines, newspapers, and your textbooks to find a wide assortment of graphic organizers. State the main purpose or type of information given in each graphic organizer.	List all the different ways you can think of that we use graphic organizers in our everyday lives. Consider how they are used in department stores, in airports, in supermarkets, and in sports.	Define graphic organizers using your own words, then use a dictionary. Compare the two definitions.	Take the information in one of the graphic organizers and rewrite it in another form.	Classify your collection of graphic organizers in at least three different ways. Explain the rationale for your grouping.
Comprehension Application Analysis	Compare a chart and a table. In a good paragraph, summarize how they are alike and how they are different.	Collect information about junk foods popular with your age group. Use a Venn Diagram to show your results.	Construct a Flow Chart to show how you would like to spend a perfect 24-hour day.	Survey the students in your class to determine their favorite television show. Show your results on a graphic organizer.	How is a graphic organizer like a road map? Like a blueprint? Like a photograph?
Analysis Synthesis	Study your collection of graphic organizers. Determine some types of data and subject matter that are best depicted by a graphic organizer.	Diagram a flow chart for constructing a graph or a table on grade point averages for students in your math class.	Write a story that has one of the following titles: "The Magic Web" "Who Needs A Concept Map?" "Who Moved My Graphic Organizer?"	Draw a picture or write a paragraph to illustrate one of these expressions: "He turned the tables on me!" "It's time to chart your course."	Design a poster about a school project, event, or activity that uses a graphic organizer as part of its message.
Evaluation	Develop a set of recommendations for students to follow when constructing a high-quality graphic organizer.	Develop a set of criteria for judging the worth or value of a given graphic organizer. Apply this criteria to each unit of your collection. Rank order your graphic organizers, from most effective to least effective.	Defend this statement: Presenting a graphic organizer is the best way to convince a friend of something.	Design a poster of graphic organizers. Find as many different examples as you can. Mount examples on poster board and write three insightful questions about each one.	Explain how each of the following people might use graphic organizers in their work: computer programmer, teacher, mall manager, astronaut, brain surgeon, and carpenter.

Standards-Based LANGUAGE ARTS Graphic Organizers, Rubrics, and Writing Prompts for Middle Grade Students

A Calendar of Writing Prompts to Encourage Writing Across the Curriculum

1 Design a graphic organizer to use for planning a class field trip. Use it to plan the trip.

2 Use multiplication facts to write an original jingle.

3 Write a letter to the chairman of the school board supporting authentic assessment as opposed to traditional testing.

4 Make up a new recipe for green peas. Give three good reasons for eating green peas at least once a week.

5 Design a kite to fly over the ocean on a very windy day. Write a paragraph describing your design.

6 Write six high-order thinking skills questions about a subject of interest to you. List the resources you will use to find answers to your questions.

7 List as many uses as you can think of for a brown paper bag.

8 Write a true story entitled "The absolute worst homework assignment I ever had and what I learned from it."

9 Write six questions with answers for a "How well do you know your community?" television special.

10 Design a word find puzzle using only weather-related words.

11 Write a paragraph telling what life would be like without calendars to help us keep track of time.

12 Create a "word-a-day" calendar for next month. Select the most interesting words you can think of to add to your vocabulary.

13 List as many rhyming word pairs as you can in three minutes. Use the rhyming pairs and only three other words to write a poem.

14 Select one of the fairy tales that you remember well and write an entirely different ending for it.

15 Compare and contrast the usefulness of a calendar and a clock; use a Venn diagram to show the likenesses and differences.

16 Design a rubric for evaluating a script for a radio program promoting a non-smoking policy for all public buildings in your community.

17 Give an example of a situation in which you would need each of the following listening skills: attentive listening, analytical listening, appreciative listening, and marginal listening.

18 Visualize, describe, and draw a series of three sketches to advertise a new miracle cake mix that includes all needed ingredients with the exception of water.

19 Design a quick and easy editor's checklist for use by students in completing assignments in content areas as well as for creative writing.

20 Design a quick and easy study guide for people learning to use English as a second language. Give rules and examples as simply and concisely as possible.

Standards-Based LANGUAGE ARTS Graphic Organizers, Rubrics, and Writing Prompts for Middle Grade Students

Performance, Project, or Task Independent Study Contract

Title: _____

Topic: _____

Beginning date of work_____

Planned completion/delivery date _____

Goals and/or learning objectives to be accomplished _____
_____

Statement of problems to be researched/studied _____
_____

Format _____

Information/data/resources needed _____
_____

Technical help needed_____
_____

Special equipment and/or materials needed _____
_____

Visual aids and/or artifacts planned _____
_____

Intended audience_____

Method of assessment _____

Student Signature _____ Date: _____

Teacher Signature _____ Date: _____

Standards-Based LANGUAGE ARTS Graphic Organizers, Rubrics, and Writing Prompts for Middle Grade Students

Bloom's Taxonomy of Cognitive Thinking Skills for Students

Bloom's Taxonomy of Cognitive Development is a model that can help you learn how to think critically and systematically. (*Taxonomy* is another word for *structure* or *schemata*.) This taxonomy provides a way to organize thinking skills into six levels. The first level is the most basic, or simplest, level of thinking, and the last level is the most challenging, or most complex, level of thinking.

BLOOM'S TAXONOMY OF CRITICAL THINKING SKILLS

KNOWLEDGE LEVEL:
> Students thinking at this level are asked to memorize, remember, and recall previously learned material. Some common verbs or behaviors for this level are: define, list, identify, label, name, recall, record, draw, recite, and reproduce.

COMPREHENSION LEVEL:
> Students thinking at this level are asked to demonstrate their ability to understand the meaning of material learned and to express that meaning in their own words. Some common verbs or behaviors for this level are: explain, describe, summarize, give examples, classify, find, measure, prepare, re-tell, reword, rewrite, and show.

APPLICATION LEVEL:
> Students thinking at this level are asked to use learned material in a situation different from the situation in which the material was taught. Some common verbs or behaviors for this level are: apply, compute, construct, develop, discuss, generalize, interview, investigate, model, perform, plan, present, produce, prove, solve, and use.

ANALYSIS LEVEL:
> Students thinking at this level are asked to break down material (ideas and concepts) into its component parts so that the organization and relationships between parts is better recognized and understood. Some common verbs or behaviors for this level are: compare and contrast, criticize, debate, determine, diagram, differentiate, discover, draw conclusions, examine, infer, search, survey, and sort.

SYNTHESIS LEVEL:
> Students thinking at this level are asked to put together parts of the material to form a new and different whole. Synthesis is the exact opposite of analysis. Some common verbs or behaviors for this level are: build, combine, create, design, imagine, invent, make-up, produce, propose, and present.

EVALUATION LEVEL:
> Students thinking at this level are asked to judge the value of material (a statement, novel, poem, research finding, fact) for a given purpose. All judgments are to be based on a set of clearly defined criteria whose outcomes can be defended or validated. Some common verbs or behaviors for this level are: assess, critique, defend, evaluate, grade, judge, measure, rank, recommend, select, test, validate, and verify.

Bibliography

A to Z Community and Service Learning. Imogene Forte and Sandra Schurr. Nashville, Incentive Publications Inc., 1997

BASIC/Not Boring Grammar and Usage Grades 6-8+. Imogene Forte and Marge Frank. Nashville, Incentive Publications Inc., 1997

BASIC/Not Boring Reading Comprehension Grades 6-8+. Imogene Forte and Marge Frank. Nashville, Incentive Publications Inc., 1997

BASIC/Not Boring Spelling Grades 6-8+. Imogene Forte and Marge Frank. Nashville, Incentive Publications Inc., 1997

BASIC/Not Boring Study and Research Grades 6-8+. Imogene Forte and Marge Frank. Nashville, Incentive Publications Inc., 1997

BASIC/Not Boring Words and Vocabulary Grades 6-8+. Imogene Forte and Marge Frank. Nashville, Incentive Publications Inc., 1997

The Definitive Middle School Guide. Imogene Forte and Sandra Schurr. Nashville, Incentive Publications Inc., 1993

Graduation Exit Exam. Darriel Ledbetter and Leland Graham. Nashville, Incentive Publications Inc., 2000

Graphic Organizers and Planning Outlines. Imogene Forte and Sandra Schurr. Nashville, Incentive Publications Inc., 1996

How to Write a Great Research Paper. Leland Graham and Darriel Ledbetter. Nashville, Incentive Publications Inc., 1994

If You're Trying to Teach Kids How to Write... You've Gotta Have This Book. Marge Frank. Nashville, Incentive Publications Inc., 1995

Integrating Instruction in Language Arts. Imogene Forte and Sandra Schurr. Nashville, Incentive Publications Inc., 1996

Interdisciplinary Units and Projects for Thematic Instruction. Nashville, Incentive Publications Inc., 1994

Reading Yellow Pages. The Kids' Stuff People. Nashville, Incentive Publications Inc., 1988

Reports Students Love to Write and Teachers Love to Read. Imogene Forte and Sandra Schurr. Nashville, Incentive Publications Inc., 1999

Use that Computer! Lucinda Johnston, Howard Johnston, and James Forde. Nashville, Incentive Publications Inc., 2001

Wow, What a Team! Randy Thompson and Dorothy VanderJagt. Nashville, Incentive Publications Inc., 2001

Writing Yellow Pages. The Kids' Stuff People. Nashville, Incentive Publications Inc., 1988

Index